Praise for *The Racial Contract*

"This is a significant and compelling work. In the modest compass of an extended essay, Mills succeeds in altering our view of a central strand of modern political thought, the social contract tradition. . . . His most accurate characterization of his enterprise comes, I believe, toward the end of the book when he places it in the tradition of radical enlightenment critique. . . . To this enterprise Mills has made a major contribution." —*Ethics*

"This is an ambitious little book, as it seeks to place race at the very center of political theory. . . . For those who agree that issues of race and racial justice demand far more attention from political theorists than they are currently receiving, the book is a welcome contribution. By showing the systematic and deeply embedded nature of racism in modern Western political theory and practice, Mills demonstrates that racist policies and ideas are not unfortunate divergences from the general rule of race neutrality but are themselves the rule in Western culture. In the process, Mills provides an analytical framework that connects claims for domestic racial justice and those for international justice. In all these respects the book is an important contribution to current discussions about justice in both realms." —*American Political Science Review*

"Charles Mills's treatment of the biases in western philosophy in *The Racial Contract* is a tour de force."
—Award Statement, Gustavus Myers Center for the Study of Bigotry and Human Rights in North America

"To take the arguments that Mills makes in *The Racial Contract* seriously is to be prepared to rethink the concept of race and the structure of our political systems. This is a very important book indeed, and should be a welcome addition to the ongoing discussions surrounding social contract theory. . . . It would be an excellent critical complement to any course that covers the history of social contract theory or that deals with issues surrounding race and racism."
—*Teaching Philosophy*

The Racial Contract

CHARLES W. MILLS

The Racial Contract

Twenty-Fifth Anniversary Edition

CORNELL UNIVERSITY PRESS
ITHACA AND LONDON

First edition published 1997 by Cornell University Press

First printed in paperback 1999

Twenty-fifth anniversary printing with new material 2022

Printed in the United States of America

Library of Congress Cataloging-in-Publication Data

Names: Mills, Charles W. (Charles Wade), author.
Title: The racial contract / Charles W. Mills.
Description: Twenty-fifth anniversary edition. |
    Ithaca [New York]: Cornell University Press, 2022. |
    Includes bibliographical references and index. |
Identifiers: LCCN 2021053910 (print) | LCCN 2021053911 (ebook) |
    ISBN 9781501764271 (hardcover) | ISBN 9781501764288 (paperback) |
    ISBN 9781501764301 (pdf) | ISBN 9781501764295 (epub)
Subjects: LCSH: Race relations. | Racism. | Social contract. |
    White supremacy movements. | Political science—Philosophy.
Classification: LCC HT1523 .M56 2022 (print) | LCC HT1523 (ebook) |
    DDC 305.8—dc23/eng/20211105
LC record available at https://lccn.loc.gov/2021053910
LC ebook record available at https://lccn.loc.gov/2021053911

This book is dedicated to the
blacks, reds, browns, and yellows
who have resisted the Racial Contract
and the white renegades and race traitors
who have refused it

CONTENTS

Contents

ACKNOWLEDGMENTS

The history that inspires this short book goes back a long way, and I have been thinking about that history, and how to incorporate it into a philosophical framework, for a long time. Along the way I have incurred many debts, some of which I have certainly forgotten, and this list of acknowledgments is only partial.

First of all, of course, to my family: my parents, Gladstone and Winnifred Mills, who brought me up to give equal respect to people of all races; my brother, Raymond Mills, and my cousin, Ward Mills, for consciousness-raising; my uncle and aunt, Don and Sonia Mills, for their role in Jamaica's own 1970s struggle against the legacy of the global Racial Contract. My wife, Elle Mills, has supported my work from the outset, sometimes having greater faith in me than I had in myself.

Special friends, past and present, should also be cited: thanks to Bobs, for old times' sake; to Lois, a friend indeed, and a friend in deed; to Femi, fellow Third Worlder, for numerous conversations since our days in grad school together about how philosophy in the academy could be made less academic.

Horace Levy, my first philosophy teacher, and for many years the mobile one-person philosophy unit of the Mona campus of the University of the West Indies, deserves particular mention, as do Frank Cunningham and Danny Goldstick of the University of Toronto, who welcomed me to the Philosophy Department graduate program there more years ago than any of us cares to remember. John Slater's confidence in me and support of my candidacy, despite my almost nonexistent undergraduate background in the subject, were crucial. To all of them, I am obligated.

I originally started working on these issues on a 1989 junior faculty summer research fellowship at the University of Oklahoma. A first draft was written in my 1993–1994 year as a Fellow of the Institute for the Humanities, University of Illinois at Chicago (UIC), and the final draft was completed during my sabbatical in the spring term of 1997. At both my previous and my present institution, I have been fortunate to have had a series of Chairs who have been very supportive of applications for grants, fellowships, travel, leave, and sabbaticals: John Biro and Kenneth Merrill at the University of Oklahoma; Richard Kraut, Dorothy Grover, and Bill Hart at UIC. Let me say how deeply grateful I am to them for that support. In addition, I have made endless requests for assistance from Charlotte Jackson and Valerie McQuay, the UIC Philosophy Department's invaluable administrative assistants, and they have been endlessly patient and helpful, greatly facilitating my work.

I thank Bernard Boxill, Dave Schweickart, and Robert Paul Wolff for their letters of endorsement for my application for the UIC Humanities Institute Fellowship that enabled me to begin the original manuscript. It was Bob Wolff's suggestion, seconded by Howard McGary Jr., that I go for "a short, punchy book" that would be accessible to an audience of nonphilosophers. Hope this is punchy enough for you, guys.

An earlier and shorter version of this book was read and critiqued by members of the Politically Correct Discussion Group of Chicago (PCDGC); I have benefited from the criticisms of Sandra Bartky, Holly Graff, David Ingram, and Olufemi Taiwo. Jay Drydyk read the manuscript and gave valuable input and encouragement. I have also benefited from audience feedback at the following presentations, from 1994 to 1996: the Institute for the Humanities, UIC; the Society for the Humanities, Cornell University; a colloquium at Queen's University; a panel at the annual meeting of the Society for Phenomenology and Existential Philosophy; and a conference titled "The Academy and Race" at Villanova University.

I have consistently received special encouragement in the project from feminist theorists: my friend Sandra Bartky, Paola Lortie, Sandra Harding, Susan Babbitt, Susan Campbell, and Iris Marion Young. I have also learned a great deal over the years from feminist political theory and obviously owe a debt to Carole Pateman in particular. My focus on race in this book should not be taken to imply that I do not recognize the reality of gender as another system of domination.

Alison Shonkwiler, my editor at Cornell University Press, was highly enthusiastic about the manuscript from her very first reading of it, and it is in large measure her conviction that persuaded me there was indeed a book here, and that I should write it. For her energy and drive, and the keen editorial eye that has undoubtedly made this a better book than it would otherwise have been, I express my deep appreciation.

Finally, as a stranger in a strange land, I have been welcomed here by the American Philosophical Association Committee on the Status of Blacks in Philosophy. I would like to single out and thank Howard McGary Jr., Leonard Harris, Lucius Outlaw Jr., Bill Lawson, Bernard Boxill, and Laurence

Thomas, for making me feel at home. As a beneficiary of affirmative action, I would not be in the American academy today were it not for the struggles of black Americans. This book is in part a tribute to, and a recognition of, those struggles, and, more generally, of the international black radical tradition of political resistance that they exemplify.

C. W. M.

1997

ACKNOWLEDGMENTS TO THE TWENTY-FIFTH ANNIVERSARY EDITION

I would like to express my appreciation to all the teachers over the years who have assigned *The Racial Contract* in innumerable courses both within and outside philosophy, across the United States and in many other countries as well. At a time (now past) when "postraciality" and "color-blindness" were emerging as the new norms, you recognized that although a postracial world may indeed be desirable, wishing does not make it so. The acknowledgment of the realities of race, and the education of the younger generation about those realities, are crucial. In doing so, you helped to make *The Racial Contract* an academic bestseller—more than fifty thousand copies sold as of 2021.

Thanks also to those of my fellow black philosophers engaged in the same project, who deserve credit as pioneers in the field, helping to establish Africana philosophy and what would eventually be designated critical philosophy of race long before they were deemed professionally respectable. My gratitude to all of you, especially those I know personally (too many to mention), both for welcoming me here to the United States and for all the years hanging out at ill-attended late-night American Philosophical Association meeting panels on race. In the end it was worth it.

I have been fortunate to have worked with two wonderful Cornell University Press editors, Alison Shonkwiler, mentioned in the original acknowledgments, and Emily Andrew. As I write this, Emily is leaving Cornell to pursue professional opportunities elsewhere. But I am in her debt for her coming up with the great idea of a twenty-fifth anniversary edition and pushing determinedly against my natural inertia to see it completed before she departed. If this new edition owes its existence to anybody, it is to you, Emily. A sincere and grateful thank you, and best wishes for your new career.

Finally, by a perfect serendipity, I was informed as we were going to press that *The Racial Contract* had just won the 2021 Benjamin E. Lippincott Award, an American Political Science Association prize given every two years to a political work "of exceptional quality by a living political theorist that is still considered significant after a time span of at least fifteen years since the original date of publication." My deep appreciation to the award committee for the honor: Barbara Arneil, chair (University of British Columbia); Steven B. Smith (Yale University); and David Runciman (University of Cambridge). I could not have wished for a better launching for this new edition.

C. W. M.

2021

FOREWORD

Tommie Shelby

Charles Mills's *The Racial Contract* (1997) is a landmark text that sought to bring about a conceptual renovation of political philosophy by placing the study of race at its center. Yet this contemporary classic is not how I first became acquainted with Mills's thought. While doing research on my dissertation in the early 1990s, I came upon several articles by Mills on a similar topic. I was trying to understand Marx's materialist critique of morality and its implications for his charge that capitalism is inherently exploitative. Mills had published essays investigating Marx's concept of ideology, historical materialism, and the limits of moral critiques of capitalist society. This scholarship greatly impressed me, and the fact that it was written in the idiom of analytic philosophy (my preferred mode of philosophical writing) made it especially congenial. I also learned around this time that Mills was black, which led me to search for his other writings, and I discovered his early papers on race and Africana philosophy.[1]

Why did Mills's racial identity matter to me? Before I entered graduate school, I had already been inspired by the work of Kwame Anthony Appiah, Bernard R. Boxill, Howard McGary, Bill Lawson, and Laurence Thomas. All are black analytic philosophers who had written important work on race and Africana philosophy. But these thinkers are each firmly rooted in the liberal tradition and have little interest in Marx's ideas, my primary interest at the time. I was also intensely curious about the race-class conundrum, in all its manifestations, and my starting point was Marxist theory. Mills was modeling the kind of work I wanted to do, in form and substance.

So you can imagine how delighted I was when, at an American Philosophical Association Meeting in the mid-1990s, I finally met the man. After a panel on which Mills was featured, he introduced himself to me. He was encouraging, supportive, and generous with his time, though I was a mere graduate student. We quickly bonded over our mutual scholarly interests and our hope to expand the intellectual space and enhance the professional environment for blacks in philosophy. When I was just starting out in the profession, he provided the kind of mentorship I have since sought to emulate with graduate students I've met or supervised. In time, Mills and I became not only colleagues but friends—sharing ideas and stories over meals, debating hard issues into the night, and working together to help grow a field we both love.

---

1. These early essays can be found in Charles W. Mills, *Blackness Visible: Essays on Philosophy and Race* (Ithaca, N.Y.: Cornell University Press, 1998) and Charles W. Mills, *From Class to Race: Essays in White Marxism and Black Radicalism* (Lanham, Md.: Rowman & Littlefield, 2003).

A lot has changed in the discipline of philosophy since we first met. Questions about race and black life have moved from the margins closer (though not quite) to the center, in large measure owing to Mills's tireless and remarkable efforts. Yet I still recall my excitement in 1997 when I got my hands on the newly published book he had been telling me about, which he signed, "To Tommie. In the conceptual struggle!" Thus, it is a tremendous honor and pleasure to write this foreword for the twenty-fifth anniversary edition of that now justly famous book.

The virtues of *The Racial Contract* are many. Rather than focus narrowly on North America and Europe (as is common), it offers a truly global perspective on race, with attention to Africa, Asia, Latin America, the Caribbean, the Pacific Islands, and Australia. It avoids, indeed breaks with, the misleading black-white binary and considers forms of racial domination where people of African descent are not the primary victims. The book is rooted in an extraordinary grasp of modern world history. Although a work of philosophy, it takes a broadly interdisciplinary approach to its subject, drawing on scholarship across the humanities and social sciences. It is also written in "punchy" and accessible prose, making it an excellent choice for undergraduate course adoption. These virtues, I believe, partly account for the book's broad appeal outside of philosophy and beyond the borders of the United States.

With respect to academic philosophy specifically, Mills charges the discipline, and political philosophy in particular, with being conceptually "white" and evasive about racial subjugation. Indeed, he has turned white supremacy into a serious philosophical subject, while castigating leaders in the field for obscuring the significance of white rule in ostensibly democratic societies. He makes a compelling case that a Racial Contract is the unacknowledged but taken-for-granted subtext of the social contract tradition—as exemplified by Hobbes, Locke, Rousseau, and Kant—which has had an enormous influence on contemporary political theory. He also charges that political philosophers have largely operated with a racialized moral psychology that distorted their theorizing and limited the applicability of their conclusions to our world. Exposing the subtle workings of the Racial Contract is then a kind of cognitive therapy for the subfield.

This attack on mainstream political philosophy should not be read as cynical irony, pessimistic resignation, or radical posturing. Its aims are ultimately emancipatory and rooted in hope for concrete structural change. Nor is it based on the fashionable dismissal and trashing of liberal political thought. Rather, Mills seeks to revise, deracialize, and radicalize liberalism so that it can be put to liberatory ends. The focus on the Racial Contract as global in scope helps us to reframe debates in political philosophy since Hobbes. Racial domination and European imperialism should, all along, have been at the center of the subfield's concerns.

Mills made a public break with traditional "white" Marxism with this book, situating his subsequent writings in the black radical tradition. Nevertheless, one can readily see the influence of Marx's ideas in the analysis offered. There is a strong stand of historical materialism and class analysis in the theses he develops. For instance, the Racial Contract is said to be driven primarily by economic gain and capital accumulation—the exploitation of land, labor, and natural resources. The approach has much in common with ideology-critique in the Western Marxist sense familiar from critical theory.

An account of how global white solidarity opposes freedom struggles from the darker peoples—a core Du Boisian theme—is articulated in the book. This is not merely about a noxious social identity but about the political and material dimensions of a transnational and catastrophic set of practices. It's as much about power, labor, money, and who lives or dies as it is about the politics of recognition and multiculturalism. The book also opens up space for and makes more legible the contributions of nonwhite political theorists, and it highlights the philosophical significance of practical antiracist struggle. The objects of this oppositional theory and practice are racial polities and global white supremacy, made more visible and explicit through Mills's provocative framework, which riffs on dominant tropes and motifs in the field.

There is currently a right-wing and, arguably, white nationalist attack on critical race theory (CRT). Most of this reactionary propaganda uses the idea of critical race theory as an empty signifier, deployed in bad faith to achieve political advantage in a period of racial polarization. *The Racial Contract* is self-consciously a contribution to critical race theory and so may help open-minded readers to better understand this intellectual movement.[2]

Pioneers of critical race theory, such as Derrick Bell, emphasized the recalcitrance and pervasiveness of racism in U.S. society. The structural foundations of the social order—from constitutional law to the criminal justice system—are thought to be rooted in white supremacy, making fundamental change extremely difficult if not impossible. What progressive change that is feasible occurs only

---

2. Some important early writings in the movement can be found in Kimberlé Crenshaw, Neil Gotanda, Gary Peller, and Kendall Thomas, eds., *Critical Race Theory: The Key Writings That Formed the Movement* (New York: The New Press, 1995).

when most white people are convinced such change will materially benefit them. Race is real and powerful but also socially constructed (not a biological kind) and sustained by legal practice. Although Mills does not treat racism as a permanent feature of U.S. society, he does regard it as foundational, issuing in what he calls a "racial polity," which was created by an agreement among those constructed as white for purposes of holding power over and exploiting those deemed not white. This Racial Contract, according to Mills, creates the construct of race and its enduring associated identities. State power is frequently used to enforce the terms of the agreement and to defeat challenges to it from racial subordinates.

Proponents of CRT are deeply critical of liberal thought and legal practice, particularly for its endorsement of color-blind social policy and for its lack of racial realism. Mills is also sharply critical of liberal theory for similar reasons. He believes that it conceals the dark history of racial domination (which continues to shape our present) by retreating into an abstract and idealistic mythology instead of confronting the concrete legacy of the global Racial Contract.

Critical race theory has developed in tandem with radical feminist theory, with its commitment to intersectionality and standpoint theory. Mills's book was inspired by the influential feminist book *The Sexual Contract* by Carole Pateman, and he incorporates key insights from radical feminism, including the idea that patriarchy is a political system in its own right and that, like the racial polity, must be dismantled. He also defends the idea that the racially oppressed have special insight into the nature of their subordination and even suggests that he is merely making such insight explicit—consider the epigraph of this book, attributed to a "black American folk aphorism."

Finally, critical race theorists, rather than rely exclusively on widely accepted modes of theoretical expression (for instance, the systematic treatise and staid journal article) or strictly conform to disciplinary norms, deploy unconventional, even transgressive, ways of communicating their ideas, including storytelling, autobiography, and allegories. Mills provides a sweeping counternarrative that upsets our expectations about what a work of political philosophy should be like.

It's not for me to say what the enduring ideas from *The Racial Contract* will be. However, there are certain ideas that have stuck with me over the last twenty-five years. To mark the peculiar form of dehumanization that people of color have experienced because of white supremacy, Mills makes a crucial distinction between a person and a subperson. Readers should pay close attention to how this distinction is developed and used to explain the relationship between the overt social contract and the covert Racial Contract.

The provocative and illuminating idea that the Racial Contract is being continuously rewritten is an underappreciated aspect of Mills's theory. The racial polity is not static but evolves with changing social conditions and shifts in power. For the most part, white dominance is no longer formally codified in law. But the contract among those who embrace their whiteness and are keen to hold on to its advantages has been redrafted to secure similar ends and to exploit the legacy of previous, more explicitly racist regimes. This makes antiracist struggle more complex and challenging, in part because many whites deny that racism continues to live.

I also believe Mills's distinction between a signatory and a beneficiary of the Racial Contract is important. Although he thinks that all whites inevitably benefit from the Racial Contract (whether they want to or not), he holds that only some whites have effectively signed on to maintain the contract. Some of these signatories openly defend white supremacist ideas and actively work to deny people of color their basic rights. Other signatories, though not (officially) subscribing to racist ideals, willingly accept the advantages of their whiteness and do little or nothing to help dismantle the racial polity. Mills is not condemning people for simply being white; nor does he think the passive acceptance of the benefits of white supremacy, in itself, makes one blameworthy. He is calling attention to complicity in regimes of racial dominance, a complicity that sometimes takes the form of indifference to and willful ignorance of past and continuing racial subordination. But the other, more hopeful, side of this point is that white people who have become conscious of the Racial Contract can refuse to sign on, can rebel against those who choose to maintain and seek to benefit from it. They can join with the darker peoples of the globe in the glorious if protracted fight to void the contract.

Although I agree with many of the criticisms Mills raises against political philosophy, I must confess that I do not endorse them all. In particular, I don't accept his critique of ideal theory, at least not in all its details. However, this is not the place to pursue our disagreements.[3] Yet there is one criticism I used to have of this book that I now think is misplaced. Mills exaggerates the flaws and failures of contemporary political philosophy. This is still my considered judgment. But I now suspect that such hyperbole was needed to draw attention to a subject so woefully and inexcusably neglected in the subfield. Perhaps it was necessary to treat the cognitive bias and blind spots that Mills correctly

---

3. See my "Racial Realities and Corrective Justice: A Reply to Charles Mills," *Critical Philosophy of Race* 1, no. 2 (2013): 145–62.

identified in the discipline. After all, Mills was attempting to effect a gestalt shift and to unsettle a reigning paradigm. Moreover, Mills was using a subversive technique drawn from the black vernacular practice of humor and comedic performance, poking fun at the dominant group and the powerful through the use of overstatement and generalizations. He was writing against the grain, against mainstream expectations and even sometimes transgressing academic norms.

These polemical strategies and this black rhetorical flair paid off, creating a classic text that has already influenced more than a generation of thinkers reflecting on the limits of mainstream political theory and the ongoing problem of racism. It is clear to me now that Mills has a distinctive voice with the power to reach many. So I welcome this new anniversary edition of *The Racial Contract*. And I sincerely hope that it provokes even more philosophers (and others so inclined) to join the conceptual struggle.

PREFACE

The Racial Contract:
What's Old Is New Again

P rofessor Mills, I'm just writing to tell you that *The Racial Contract* changed my life."

Mine too.

I've received many such letters over the years from students of color who emailed me out of the blue to let me know about the impact my book had had on them. *The Racial Contract* struck a chord, one that still resonates decades later. Indeed, considering that I am writing this in the wake of the massive global demonstrations against racism sparked by the death of George Floyd at the hands of the Minneapolis police, its greatest influence may yet lie ahead. A book that begins with the seemingly provocative statement "White supremacy is the unnamed political system that has made the modern world what it is today," no longer seems as outrageous. International protests against the legacy of European colonialism, imperialism, racial slavery, and exclusionary white settler states; demands to reform Western curricula and educational systems that foster a dangerous "white ignorance" about the past and the present; calls for an end to structural white domination and racial injustice—suddenly it has become much harder to deny the accuracy of the picture painted by this short book twenty-five years ago.

I am following a long line of black intellectuals, working in numerous disciplines, who have hoped that their writings would help to create a better society. In philosophy, there are many conceptions of philosophers and the philosophical task, from humble under-laborer (Locke) to ambitious system-builder (Hegel), from a discipline that leaves everything as it is (Wittgenstein) to one that aims to change the world (Marx). But the international black radical tradition has always been unwaveringly committed to the latter.[4] Long before the birth of Karl Marx, the forced diaspora of African slavery had given rise to a community of the racially oppressed seeking to critically analyze, understand, and ultimately end their oppression. In Leonard Harris's formulation, African American philosophy (and, in significant measure, modern Africana philosophy) is a "philosophy born of struggle."[5] The classroom and the conference panel are relatively recent locational settings of this revolutionary discourse; the original milieu was the slaves' quarters. And at its best, the black radical tradition has not been narrowly nationalist but has declared its solidarity with the subordinated everywhere.

---

4. Cedric J. Robinson's *Black Marxism: The Making of the Black Radical Tradition* (Chapel Hill, N.C.: University of North Carolina Press, 2000) originally coined the phrase, though its content remains contested.
5. Leonard Harris, ed., *Philosophy Born of Struggle: Anthology of Afro-American Philosophy from 1917* (Dubuque, Iowa: Kendall/Hunt, 1983).

So unlike those mainstream white philosophers, particularly in the analytic tradition, who present themselves as disinterested thinkers addressing timeless issues without any need for attention to contingent circumstance, I see the discipline as embodied and socially embedded. The Racial Contract is shaped both by the black experience and my specific identity as a Jamaican, then as a Jamaican-American, after I immigrated to the United States, to become part of the tiny but resolute group of black philosophers (still at just 1 percent of the profession).

The international perspective manifest in the book came readily to me. If you're from a small Global South nation of fewer than three million people, it's harder to believe that you're at the center of the world (though some Jamaicans have given it the old college try) and to ignore the international forces that have determined the contours of that world. Indeed, the very formation of Jamaica in the modern period is the result of European imperialism. Xaymaca (the original Taino Amerindian name) was invaded and conquered by Christopher Columbus in 1494. The indigenous population was decimated, and a slave economy established through the importation of captured African peoples. The Spanish were later driven out by the British in the 1650s and large-scale slavery instituted, making the country one of Britain's most profitable slave possessions (an "exploitation colony" to which whites were basically external overseers, as against the European white settler colonies, like the United States, marked by massive European immigration). Slavery was finally abolished over the course of four years beginning in 1834, but Jamaica would remain a British colony until 1962. And racist ideologies of European superiority justified these systems of domination throughout hundreds of years.

Not surprisingly, then, the newly independent Jamaica in which I was raised was absorbed in intense political debates over the issue of colonialism and its legacy for postcolonial (or was that really neocolonial?) Jamaica. Moreover, under the 1970s social-democratic government of Michael Manley, Jamaica was not just trying to reform its inherited white/brown/black pyramidal socioeconomic structure but also playing a key role on the global stage; along with other Global South nations, it attempted to create a New International Economic Order. Leaving this hothouse political atmosphere, steeped in the radical Anglo-Caribbean debates of the time, I was therefore completely astonished to be introduced to mainstream political philosophy in the work of John Rawls when I started my PhD at the University of Toronto. His injunction, in *A Theory of Justice*, that we should think of society as actually—not merely ideally— being "a cooperative venture for mutual advantage" whose rules are "designed to advance the good of those taking part in it" made me realize that these people were working with a very different playbook![6]

Although written many years later, *The Racial Contract* should be viewed as my emphatic refusal of any such conceptualization. In effect, I wrote the book I would have liked to read myself when first trying to negotiate the blinding whiteness of the discipline. (The many students who email me are still facing the same problem.) This whiteness has to be understood not merely in terms of numbers and professional demography, not just as manifest in racist comments about people of color in the work of canonical figures and

---

6. John Rawls, *A Theory of Justice*, rev. ed. (Cambridge, Mass.: Harvard University Press, 1999), p. 4.

the exclusion of people of color from that same canon, but—
at its most profound and challenging level—in the conceptual and theoretical framing of key issues. And in terms of
reaching a mass audience for my own attempted reframing,
The Racial Contract is my success story, having sold several times more than my other five books combined, and
constituting almost half of my total citations on Google
Scholar. Its uptake has been both international and interdisciplinary. It has been applied, I've been told, to comparative
color hierarchies in Jamaica and Barbados, politics in postcolonial India, the national and international racial dynamics
of Israel/Palestine, racism in the Australian Public Service,
and "white ignorance" in the New Zealand (Aotearoa) educational system. It has been widely adopted in classrooms
across disciplines outside philosophy: political science, sociology, education, international relations, African American
studies, anthropology, history, and the law.

Having completed my doctoral work in Canada, I would
eventually secure a job in the United States, joining a committed cohort of black philosophers, largely African American, who'd long been engaged in the same project.

It is difficult to convey to today's younger readers how
different the philosophical scene was in the mid-1990s.
Books on race and African American philosophy were being
published—dealing with social justice, the prophetic religious tradition, the problem of the "underclass," philosophy
and slavery, and African American philosophical traditions—
but they were still comparatively rare. Not a single publisher
had a philosophy and race or African American philosophy
series; today at least five do. Nor were there any companions
or guidebooks to either field; now there are at least three.

But Kwame Anthony Appiah's *In My Father's House*,
which appeared in 1992, provided a turning point of sorts,

though it was not necessarily recognized as such at the time.[7] In the view of fellow black philosopher Paul C. Taylor, Appiah's book was the crucial text in legitimating the study of race and Africana philosophy for the mainstream. Not only did Appiah have impeccable Oxbridge credentials but he also had a technical background in analytic philosophy of language. Because, for better or worse, analytic philosophy is the hegemonic approach in the profession, it meant that race and Africana were thereby made respectable in a way that Continental treatments would not have been able to accomplish. But although Appiah's work reached a much larger audience, his conclusions were unwelcome to most black philosophers. His position on race was famously eliminativist—"The truth is that there are no races"—and he was hostile to the race-based Pan-Africanist political tradition, for example in the writings of W. E. B. Du Bois, as morally dubious and possibly even racist.[8] By contrast, Lucius Outlaw, coming from the Continental Critical Theory tradition (though critical of it for neglecting race) and long involved in the black American liberation struggle, was insistent on race's reality and sociopolitical significance, articulated in his book, *On Philosophy and Race*.[9] In the small philosophical circles of people interested in race, the Appiah-Outlaw quarrel would be recognized as the key debate of the period, played out in panels and journal articles, not to mention a dramatic blowup at

---

7. Kwame Anthony Appiah, *In My Father's House: Africa in the Philosophy of Culture* (New York: Oxford University Press, 1992).
8. Appiah, *In My Father's House*, p. 40. In subsequent work, he would somewhat modify his original position.
9. Lucius T. Outlaw, *On Philosophy and Race* (New York: Routledge, 1996).

the 1994 Rutgers philosophy and race conference (though peace and civility were later restored—ask your elders for the details).

Naturally, I wanted to join this conversation myself, but how exactly? My own sympathies were definitely with Outlaw, if not with his idiom. I was trained as an analytic philosopher and continue to regard myself as such, though my openness to insights from history, sociology, political science—and that slice of Continental philosophy I can understand—has made me suspect, or perhaps simply renegade, to many analytic eyes. The challenge, as I saw it, was to make analytic political philosophy more socio-historically responsible: how could this be accomplished? *The Racial Contract* can be thought of as a black philosophical intervention that takes the eminently respectable political apparatus of social contract theory and tries to adapt it in a radical way so as to bring race into the picture. Instead of the segregated white discourse of the mainstream analytic political philosophy of the time, I was arguing for a new framing that acknowledged the political realities marking the experience of people of color in modernity. Yes, race does indeed exist, if not biologically, then as a social construct with a social reality, and yes, race in general and white domination in particular have been central to making the modern world, and so yes, we can—and we should—develop a political philosophy informed by these realities, while of course itself eschewing racism.

My Jamaican roots, and Afro-Caribbean internationalist sympathies, had found a way to express themselves, in solidarity and dialogue with the black American radical tradition, in a synthesizing book (and subsequent body of work). In it, I stake out a position I have recently started calling black radical liberalism, intended as part of a broadly revisionist antiracist rethinking of liberalism for progressives.[10] And indeed Tommie Shelby, author of the foreword to this edition of my book, suggests in his book, *Dark Ghettos: Injustice, Dissent, and Reform*, that while given different names, this is a position, or a cluster of positions, historically adopted by many black political thinkers.[11] Although Shelby and I may disagree on the details, particularly our readings of Rawls, we agree on the big picture. (For a parallel from the world of gender studies, think of the many different varieties of feminist liberalism.)[12] The idea is to retrieve liberalism in a race-sensitive form, taking into account black feminist critiques. Shatema Threadcraft's work, for example, emphasizes the necessity of developing concepts of racial oppression and corresponding corrective racial justice that recognize the intersectional nature of both, such as the historic violation of the reproductive rights of black women.[13]

Here is my own rendition of this project. Black radical liberalism is, of necessity, intimately and critically engaged with the "white" European and Euro-American political traditions. Indeed, to speak of them as completely separate traditions runs the risk of reifying them as clearly distinct entities, mapping different territories, when of course the whole point of the black/Africana tradition is to be offering a revisionist cartography of the same territory. It is not a

10. Charles W. Mills, *Black Rights/White Wrongs: The Critique of Racial Liberalism* (New York: Oxford University Press, 2017).

11. Tommie Shelby, *Dark Ghettos: Injustice, Dissent, and Reform* (Cambridge, Mass.: Harvard University Press, 2016).

12. See, for example, Amy R. Baehr, ed., *Varieties of Feminist Liberalism* (Lanham, Md.: Rowman & Littlefield, 2004) and Ruth Abbey, *The Return of Feminist Liberalism* (New York: Routledge, 2011).

13. For a critical discussion of both Shelby and myself, see Shatema Threadcraft, *Intimate Justice: The Black Female Body and the Body Politic* (New York: Oxford University Press, 2016).

matter of different political worlds but of hegemonic and sub-
altern perspectives on the "same" political world—though
experienced and viewed very differently from the positions
of social privilege and social subordination.

Both a descriptive and a normative aspect are therefore
involved: the redrawing of standard boundaries and internal
differentiations of political space and the raising of normative
questions typically ignored or, more strongly, rejected outright by the hegemonic order. The Western liberal nations and
those countries upon whom they've imposed their liberalism,
which Rawls urges us to think of as cooperative ventures for
mutual advantage, were white supremacist states. Racism
was not an anomaly but constitutively incorporated into their
"basic structures" (to cite Rawls) as colonial and imperial
powers, exploitation colonies, societies of racial chattel slavery, and white settler states. But because white supremacy is
not acknowledged (a descriptive/conceptual evasion), racial
justice is thematically marginalized (a normative/prescriptive
evasion). The result? The white Western liberal social justice
theory of the last half-century.

My claim is, then, that as standardly deployed, the social
contract metaphor of Western political theory revived by
Rawls in the 1970s onward is not remotely a neutral apparatus for representing these realities but a tendentious and
deeply theoretically biased one. Instead, we need to work
with the competing and more useful metaphor of a "domination contract," whether for race, as in the Racial Contract,
or in other contexts.[14] We will thereby be able to engage with

---

14. Carole Pateman, *The Sexual Contract* (Palo Alto, Calif.: Stanford
University Press, 1988); Stacy Clifford Simplican, *The Capacity
Contract: Intellectual Disability and the Question of Citizenship*
(Minneapolis, Minn.: University of Minnesota Press, 2015).

the most influential strains of liberal discourse while giving voice to the people of color victimized by Western racial domination and consequent racial injustice. The question of social justice then becomes primarily a matter of corrective justice: how do we dismantle the racialized basic structure created by the Racial Contract?[15] Instead of being siloed in a separate conceptual world, the political texts of people of color rooted in their long history of antiimperialist, anticolonial, abolitionist, antiapartheid, and antiracist struggles are integrated into a discursive space that addresses all the same problems as mainstream theory but through racially informed rather than racially evasive lines of inquiry.

The anniversary edition of this book is the occasion for looking forward as well as for looking back. As I write this preface, a new generation of political philosophers and theorists is examining the problems of structural racial injustice on a global scale. A post-Floyd world cannot—one hopes— return to the political obliviousness of the past about race. I hope also that *The Racial Contract* will continue to serve as a valuable text in advancing this project. While there are reasons for optimism, a backlash against critical race theory and the critical philosophy of race is arising. Powerful political forces in various Western nations—the United States, Britain, and France, among others—see such work as subversive, threatening the existing order.[16] And in a sense, of course, they are completely correct, considering the establishment of that order on white racial domination. Their opposition

15. For my own suggestions, see my 2020 Tanner Lecture, "Theorizing Racial Justice," forthcoming in *The Tanner Lectures on Human Values*.
16. Michelle Goldberg, "The Campaign to Cancel Wokeness," *New York Times* (print), February 28, 2021, SR, 3.

confirms the validity of *The Racial Contract*'s diagnosis—
that liberalism was and is racialized, based on exclusion, and
the substantive inclusion of people of color will be resisted.
Only by admitting and confronting this reality can the Racial
Contract be unmade. The struggle for racial justice continues, but so does the struggle against it.

The Racial Contract

When white people say "Justice," they mean "Just us."

—black American folk aphorism

INTRODUCTION

White supremacy is the unnamed political system that has made the modern world what it is today. You will not find this term in introductory, or even advanced, texts in political theory. A standard undergraduate philosophy course will start off with Plato and Aristotle, perhaps say something about Augustine, Aquinas, and Machiavelli, move on to Hobbes, Locke, Mill, and Marx, and then wind up with Rawls and Nozick. It will introduce you to notions of aristocracy, democracy, absolutism, liberalism, representative government, socialism, welfare capitalism, and libertarianism. But though it covers more than two thousand years of Western political thought and runs the ostensible gamut of political systems, there will be no mention of the basic political system that has shaped the world for the past several hundred years. And this omission is not accidental. Rather, it reflects the fact that standard textbooks and courses have for the most part been written and designed by whites, who take their racial privilege so much for granted that they do not even see it as *political*, as a form of domination. Ironically, the most important political system of recent global history—the system of domination by which white people have historically ruled over and, in certain important ways, continue to rule over nonwhite people—is not seen as a political system at all. It is just taken for granted; it is the background against which other systems, which we *are* to see as political, are highlighted. This book is an attempt to redirect your vision, to make you see what, in a sense, has been there all along.

Philosophy has remained remarkably untouched by the debates over multiculturalism, canon reform, and ethnic diversity racking the academy; both demographically and conceptually, it is one of the "whitest" of the humanities. Blacks, for example, constitute only about 1 percent of philosophers in North American universities—a hundred or so people out of more than ten thousand—and there are even fewer Latino, Asian American, and Native American philosophers.[1] Surely this underrepresentation itself stands in need of an explanation, and in my opinion it can be traced in part to a conceptual array and a standard repertoire of concerns whose abstractness typically elides, rather than genuinely includes, the experience of racial minorities. Since (white) women have the demographic advantage of numbers, there are of course far more female philosophers in the profession than nonwhite philosophers (though still not proportionate to women's percentage of the population), and they have made far greater progress in developing alternative conceptualizations. Those African American philosophers who do work in moral and political theory tend either to produce general work indistinguishable from that of their white peers or to focus on local issues (affirmative action, the black "underclass") or historical figures (W. E. B. Du Bois, Alain Locke) in a way that does not aggressively engage the broader debate.

What is needed is a global theoretical framework for situating discussions of race and white racism, and thereby challenging the assumptions of white political philosophy, which

2

would correspond to feminist theorists' articulation of the centrality of gender, patriarchy, and sexism to traditional moral and political theory. What is needed, in other words, is a recognition that racism (or, as I will argue, global white supremacy) is *itself* a political system, a particular power structure of formal or informal rule, socioeconomic privilege, and norms for the differential distribution of material wealth and opportunities, benefits and burdens, rights and duties. The notion of the Racial Contract is, I suggest, one possible way of making this connection with mainstream theory, since it uses the vocabulary and apparatus already developed for contractarianism to map this unacknowledged system. Contract talk is, after all, the political lingua franca of our times.

We all understand the idea of a "contract," an agreement between two or more people to do something. The "social contract" just extends this idea. If we think of human beings as starting off in a "state of nature," it suggests that they then *decide* to establish civil society and a government. What we have, then, is a theory that founds government on the popular consent of individuals taken as equals.[2]

But the peculiar contract to which I am referring, though based on the social contract tradition that has been central to Western political theory, is not a contract between everybody ("we the people"), but between just the people who count, the people who really are people ("we the white people"). So it is a Racial Contract.

The social contract, whether in its original or in its contemporary version, constitutes a powerful set of lenses for looking at society and the government. But in its obfuscation of the ugly realities of group power and domination, it is, if unsupplemented, a profoundly misleading account of the way the modern world actually is and came to be. The "Racial Contract" as a theory—I use quotation marks to indicate when I am

3

talking about the theory of the Racial Contract, as against the Racial Contract itself—will explain that the Racial Contract is real and that apparent racist violations of the terms of the social contract in fact *uphold* the terms of the Racial Contract.

The "Racial Contract," then, is intended as a conceptual bridge between two areas now largely segregated from each other: on the one hand, the world of mainstream (i.e., white) ethics and political philosophy, preoccupied with discussions of justice and rights in the abstract, on the other hand, the world of Native American, African American, and Third and Fourth World[3] political thought, historically focused on issues of conquest, imperialism, colonialism, white settlement, land rights, race and racism, slavery, jim crow, reparations, apartheid, cultural authenticity, national identity, *indigenismo*, Afrocentrism, etc. These issues hardly appear in mainstream political philosophy,[4] but they have been central to the political struggles of the majority of the world's population. Their absence from what is considered serious philosophy is a reflection not of their lack of seriousness but of the color of the vast majority of Western academic philosophers (and perhaps *their* lack of seriousness).

The great virtue of traditional social contract theory was that it provided seemingly straightforward answers both to factual questions about the origins and workings of society and government and to normative questions about the justification of socioeconomic structures and political institutions. Moreover, the "contract" was very versatile, depending on how different theorists viewed the state of nature, human motivation, the rights and liberties people gave up or retained, the particular details of the agreement, and the resulting character of the government. In the modern Rawlsian version of the contract, this flexibility continues to be illustrated, since Rawls dispenses with the historical claims of classic contractarianism and focuses instead on the justification of the basic structure of society.[5] From its 1650–1800 heyday as a grand quasi-anthropological account of the origins and development of society and the state, the contract has now become just a normative tool, a conceptual device to elicit our intuitions about justice.

But my usage is different. The "Racial Contract" I employ is in a sense more in keeping with the spirit of the classic contractarians—Hobbes, Locke, Rousseau, and Kant.[6] I use it not merely normatively, to generate judgments about social justice and injustice, but descriptively, to *explain* the actual genesis of the society and the state, the way society is structured, the way the government functions, and people's moral psychology.[7] The most famous case in which the contract is used to explain a manifestly *non*ideal society, what would be termed in current philosophical jargon a "naturalized" account, is Rousseau's *Discourse on Inequality* (1755). Rousseau argues that technological development in the state of nature brings into existence a nascent society of growing divisions in wealth between rich and poor, which are then consolidated and made permanent by a deceitful "social contract."[8] Whereas the ideal contract explains how a just society would be formed, ruled by a moral government, and regulated by a defensible moral code, this nonideal/naturalized contract explains how an unjust, *exploitative* society, ruled by an *oppressive* government and regulated by an *immoral* code, comes into existence. If the ideal contract is to be endorsed and emulated, this nonideal/naturalized contract is to be demystified and condemned. So the point of analyzing the nonideal contract is not to ratify it but to use it to explain and expose the inequities of the actual nonideal polity and to help us to see through the theories and moral justifications offered in defense of them. It gives us a kind of X-ray vision into the real internal

5

logic of the sociopolitical system. Thus it does normative work for us not through its own values, which are detestable, but by enabling us to understand the polity's actual history and how these values and concepts have functioned to rationalize oppression, so as to reform them.

Carole Pateman's provocative feminist work of a decade ago, *The Sexual Contract*, is a good example of this approach (and the inspiration for my own book, though my use is somewhat different), which demonstrates how much descriptive/explanatory life there still is in the contract.[9] Pateman uses it naturalistically, as a way of modeling the internal dynamic of the nonideal male-dominated societies that actually exist today. So this is, as indicated, a reversion to the original "anthropological" approach in which the contract *is* intended to be historically explanatory. But the twist is, of course, that her purpose is now subversive: to excavate the hidden, unjust male covenant upon which the ostensibly gender-neutral social contract actually rests. By looking at Western society and its prevailing political and moral ideologies as if they were based on an unacknowledged "Sexual Contract," Pateman offers a "conjectural history" that reveals and exposes the normative logic that makes sense of the inconsistencies, circumlocutions, and evasions of the classic contract theorists and, correspondingly, the world of patriarchal domination their work has helped to rationalize.

My aim here is to adopt a nonideal contract as a rhetorical trope and theoretical method for understanding the inner logic of *racial* domination and how it structures the polities of the West and elsewhere. The ideal "social contract" has been a central concept of Western political theory for understanding and evaluating the social world. And concepts are crucial to cognition: cognitive scientists point out that they help us to categorize, learn, remember, infer, explain, problem-solve, generalize, analogize.[10] Correspondingly, the *lack* of appropriate concepts can hinder learning, interfere with memory, block inferences, obstruct explanation, and perpetuate problems. I am suggesting, then, that as a central concept the notion of a Racial Contract might be more revealing of the real character of the world we are living in, and the corresponding historical deficiencies of its normative theories and practices, than the raceless notions currently dominant in political theory.[11] Both at the primary level of an alternative conceptualization of the facts and at the secondary (reflexive) level of a critical analysis of the orthodox theories themselves, the "Racial Contract" enables us to engage with mainstream Western political theory to bring in race. Insofar as contractarianism is thought of as a useful way to do political philosophy, to theorize about how the polity was created and what values should guide our prescriptions for making it more just, it is obviously crucial to understand what the original and continuing "contract" actually was and is, so that we can correct for it in constructing the ideal "contract." The "Racial Contract" should therefore be enthusiastically welcomed by white contract theorists as well.

So this book can be thought of as resting on three simple claims: the existential claim—white supremacy, both local and global, exists and has existed for many years; the conceptual claim—white supremacy should be thought of as itself a political system; the methodological claim—as a political system, white supremacy can illuminatingly be theorized as based on a "contract" between whites, a Racial Contract.

Here, then, are ten theses on the Racial Contract, divided into three chapters.

OVERVIEW

I will start with an overview of the Racial Contract, high-
lighting its differences from, as well as its similarities
to, the classical and contemporary social contract. The
Racial Contract is political, moral, and epistemological; the
Racial Contract is real; and economically, in determining who
gets what, the Racial Contract is an exploitation contract.

The Racial Contract is political, moral, and epistemological.

The "social contract" is actually several contracts in one.
Contemporary contractarians usually distinguish, to begin
with, between the *political* contract and the *moral* contract,
before going on to make (subsidiary) distinctions within both.
I contend, however, that the orthodox social contract also
tacitly presupposes an "epistemological" contract, and that
for the Racial Contract it is crucial to make this explicit.

The political contract is an account of the origins of government and our political obligations to it. The subsidiary distinction sometimes made in the political contract is between the
contract to establish *society* (thereby taking "natural," preso-

cial individuals out of the state of nature and reconstructing and constituting them as members of a collective body) and the contract to establish the *state* (thereby transferring outright or delegating in a relationship of trust the rights and powers we have in the state of nature to a sovereign governing entity).[1] The moral contract, on the other hand, is the foundation of the moral code established for the society, by which the citizens are supposed to regulate their behavior. The subsidiary distinction here is between two interpretations (to be discussed) of the relationship between the moral contract and state-of-nature morality. In modern versions of the contract, most notably Rawls's of course, the political contract largely vanishes, modern anthropology having long superseded the naive social origin histories of the classic contractarians. The focus is then almost exclusively on the moral contract. This is not conceived of as an actual historical event that took place on leaving the state of nature. Rather, the state of nature survives only in the attenuated form of what Rawls calls the "original position," and the "contract" is a purely hypothetical exercise (a thought experiment) in establishing what a just "basic structure" would be, with a schedule of rights, duties, and liberties that shapes citizens' moral psychology, conceptions of the right, notions of self-respect, etc.[2]

Now the Racial Contract—and the "Racial Contract" as a theory, that is, the distanced, critical examination of the Racial Contract—follows the classical model in being both sociopolitical and moral. It explains how society was created or crucially transformed, how the individuals in that society were reconstituted, how the state was established, and how a particular moral code and a certain moral psychology were brought into existence. (As I have emphasized, the "Racial Contract" seeks to account for the way things are and how they came to be that way—the descriptive—*as well as* the way they should be—the normative—since indeed one of its complaints about white political philosophy is precisely its otherworldiness, its ignoring of basic political realities.) But the Racial Contract, as we will see, is also epistemological, prescribing norms for cognition to which its signatories must adhere. A preliminary characterization would run something like this:

The Racial Contract is that set of formal or informal agreements or meta-agreements (higher-level contracts *about* contracts, which set the limits of the contracts' validity) between the members of one subset of humans, henceforth designated by (shifting) "racial" (phenotypical/genealogical/cultural) criteria C_1, C_2, C_3 . . . as "white," and coextensive (making due allowance for gender differentiation) with the class of full persons, to categorize the remaining subset of humans as "nonwhite" and of a different and inferior moral status, subpersons, so that they have a subordinate civil standing in the white or white-ruled polities the whites either already inhabit or establish or in transactions as aliens with these polities, and the moral and juridical rules normally regulating the behavior of whites in their dealings with one another either do not apply at all in dealings with nonwhites or apply only in a qualified form (depending in part on changing historical circumstances and what particular variety of nonwhite is involved), but in any case the general purpose of the Contract is always the differential privileging of the whites as a group with respect to the nonwhites as a group, the exploitation of their bodies, land, and resources, and the denial of equal socioeconomic opportunities to them. All whites are *beneficiaries* of the Contract, though some whites are not *signatories* to it.[3]

It will be obvious, therefore, that the Racial Contract is not a contract to which the nonwhite subset of humans can be a

11

genuinely consenting party (though, depending again on the circumstances, it may sometimes be politic to pretend that this is the case). Rather, it is a contract between those categorized as white *over* the nonwhites, who are thus the objects rather than the subjects of the agreement.

The logic of the classic social contract, political, moral, and epistemological, then undergoes a corresponding refraction, with shifts, accordingly, in the key terms and principles.

Politically, the contract to establish society and the government, thereby transforming abstract raceless "men" from denizens of the state of nature into social creatures who are politically obligated to a neutral state, becomes the founding of a *racial polity*, whether white settler states (where preexisting populations already are or can be made sparse) or what are sometimes called "sojourner colonies," the establishment of a white presence and colonial rule over existing societies (which are somewhat more populous, or whose inhabitants are more resistant to being made sparse). In addition, the colonizing mother country is also changed by its relation to these new polities, so that its own citizens are altered.

In the social contract, the crucial human metamorphosis is from "natural" man to "civil/political" man, from the resident of the state of nature to the citizen of the created society. This change can be more or less extreme, depending on the theorist involved. For Rousseau it is a dramatic transformation, by which animallike creatures of appetite and instinct become citizens bound by justice and self-prescribed laws. For Hobbes it is a somewhat more laid-back affair by which people who look out primarily for themselves learn to constrain their self-interest for their own good.[4] But in all cases the original "state of nature" supposedly indicates the condition of *all* men, and the social metamorphosis affects them all in the same way.

In the Racial Contract, by contrast, the crucial metamorphosis is the preliminary conceptual partitioning and corresponding transformation of human populations into "white" and "nonwhite" men. The role played by the "state of nature" then becomes radically different. In the white settler state, its role is not primarily to demarcate the (temporarily) prepolitical state of "all" men (who are really white men), but rather the permanently prepolitical state or, perhaps better, nonpolitical state (insofar as "pre-" suggests eventual internal movement toward) of nonwhite men. The establishment of society thus implies the denial that a society already existed; the creation of society *requires* the intervention of white men, who are thereby positioned as *already* sociopolitical beings. White men who are (definitionally) already part of society encounter nonwhites who are not, who are "savage" residents of a state of nature characterized in terms of wilderness, jungle, wasteland. These the white men bring partially into society as subordinate citizens or exclude on reservations or deny the existence of or exterminate. In the colonial case, admittedly preexisting but (for one reason or another) deficient societies (decadent, stagnant, corrupt) are taken over and run for the "benefit" of the nonwhite natives, who are deemed childlike, incapable of self-rule and handling their own affairs, and thus appropriately wards of the state. Here the natives are usually characterized as "barbarians" rather than "savages," their state of nature being somewhat farther away (though not, of course, as remote and lost in the past—if it ever existed in the first place—as the Europeans' state of nature). But in times of crisis the conceptual distance between the two, barbarian and savage, tends to shrink or collapse, for this technical distinction within the nonwhite population is vastly less important than the *central* distinction between whites and nonwhites.

In both cases, then, though in different ways, the Racial Contract establishes a racial polity, a racial state, and a racial juridical system, where the status of whites and nonwhites is clearly demarcated, whether by law or custom. And the purpose of this state, by contrast with the neutral state of classic contractarianism, is, inter alia, specifically to maintain and reproduce this racial order, securing the privileges and advantages of the full white citizens and maintaining the subordination of nonwhites. Correspondingly, the "consent" expected of the white citizens is in part conceptualized as a consent, whether explicit or tacit, to the racial order, to white supremacy, what could be called Whiteness. To the extent that those phenotypically/genealogically/culturally categorized as white fail to live up to the civic and political responsibilities of Whiteness, they are in dereliction of their duties as citizens. From the inception, then, race is in no way an "afterthought," a "deviation" from ostensibly raceless Western ideals, but rather a central shaping constituent of those ideals.

In the social contract tradition, there are two main possible relations between the moral contract and the political contract. On the first view, the moral contract represents *preexisting* objectivist morality (theological or secular) and thus constrains the terms of the political contract. This is the view found in Locke and Kant. In other words, there is an objective moral code in the state of nature itself, even if there are no policemen and judges to enforce it. So any society, government, and legal system that are established should be based on that moral code. On the second view, the political contract *creates* morality as a conventionalist set of rules. So there is no independent objective moral criterion for judging one moral code to be superior to another or for indicting a society's established morality as unjust. On this conception, which is famously attributed to Hobbes, morality is just a set of rules for expediting the rational pursuit and coordination of our own interests without conflict with those other people who are doing the same thing.[5]

The Racial Contract can accommodate both versions, but as it is the former version (the contract as described in Locke and Kant) rather than the latter version (the contract as described in Hobbes) which represents the mainstream of the contract tradition, I focus on that one.[6] Here, the good polity is taken to rest on a preexisting moral foundation. Obviously, this is a far more attractive conception of a political system than Hobbes's view. The ideal of an objectively just polis to which we should aspire in our political activism goes back in the Western tradition all the way to Plato. In the medieval Christian worldview which continued to influence contractarianism well into the modern period, there is a "natural law" immanent in the structure of the universe which is supposed to direct us morally in striving for this ideal.[7] (For the later, secular versions of contractarianism, the idea would simply be that people have rights and duties even in the state of nature because of their nature as human beings.) So it is wrong to steal, rape, kill in the state of nature even if there are no human laws written down saying it is wrong. These moral principles must constrain the human laws that are made and the civil rights that are assigned once the polity is established. In part, then, the political contract simply *codifies* a morality that already exists, writing it down and filling in the details, so we don't have to rely on a divinely implanted moral sense, or conscience, whose perceptions may on occasion be distorted by self-interest. What is right and wrong, just and unjust, in society will largely be determined by what is right and wrong, just and unjust, in the state of nature.

The character of this objective moral foundation is therefore obviously crucial. For the mainstream of the contractarian tradition, it is the *freedom and equality of all men in the state of nature.* As Locke writes in the *Second Treatise,* "To understand Political Power right, and derive it from its Original, we must consider what State all Men are naturally in, and that is, a *State of perfect Freedom* to order their Actions. . . . A *State* also *of Equality,* wherein all the Power and Jurisdiction is reciprocal, no one having more than another."[8] For Kant, similarly, it is our equal moral personhood.[9] Contractarianism is (supposedly) committed to moral egalitarianism, the moral equality of all men, the notion that the interests of all men matter equally and all men must have equal rights. Thus, contractarianism is also committed to a principled and foundational opposition to the traditionalist hierarchical ideology of the old feudal order, the ideology of inherent ascribed status and natural subordination. It is this language of equality which echoes in the American and French Revolutions, the Declaration of Independence, and the Declaration of the Rights of Man. And it is this moral egalitarianism that must be retained in the allocation of rights and liberties in civil society. When in a modern Western society people insist on their rights and freedoms and express their outrage at not being treated equally, it is to these classic ideas that, whether they know it or not, they are appealing.

But as we will see in greater detail later on, the color-coded morality of the Racial Contract restricts the possession of this natural freedom and equality to *white* men. By virtue of their complete nonrecognition, or at best inadequate, myopic recognition, of the duties of natural law, nonwhites are appropriately relegated to a lower rung on the moral ladder (the Great Chain of Being).[10] They are designated as born *unfree* and *unequal.* A partitioned social ontology is therefore created, a universe divided between persons and racial subpersons, *Untermenschen,* who may variously be black, red, brown, yellow— slaves, aborigines, colonial populations—but who are collectively appropriately known as "subject races." And these subpersons—niggers, injuns, chinks, wogs, greasers, blackfellows, kaffirs, coolies, abos, dinks, googoos, gooks—are biologically destined never to penetrate the normative rights ceiling established for them below white persons. Henceforth, then, whether openly admitted or not, it is taken for granted that the grand ethical theories propounded in the development of Western moral and political thought are of restricted scope, explicitly or implicitly intended by their proponents to be restricted to persons, whites. The terms of the Racial Contract set the parameters for white morality as a whole, so that competing Lockean and Kantian contractarian theories of natural rights and duties, or later anticontractarian theories such as nineteenth-century utilitarianism, are all limited by its stipulations.

Finally, the Racial Contract requires its own peculiar moral and empirical epistemology, its norms and procedures for determining what counts as moral and factual knowledge of the world. In the standard accounts of contractarianism it is not usual to speak of there being an "epistemological" contract, but there *is* an epistemology associated with contractarianism, in the form of natural law. This provides us with a moral compass, whether in the traditional version of Locke—the light of reason implanted in us by God so we can discern objective right and wrong—or in the revisionist version of Hobbes—the ability to assess the objectively optimal prudential course of action and what it requires of us for self-interested cooperation with others. So through our natural faculties we come to know reality in both its factual and valuational aspects, the way things objectively are and what is objectively good or bad about them. I suggest we can think of this as an idealized consensus about cognitive norms and, in this respect, an agreement or "contract" of sorts. There is an understanding about what counts as a correct, objective interpretation of the world, and for agreeing to this view, one is ("contractually") granted full cognitive standing in the polity, the official epistemic community.[11]

But for the Racial Contract things are necessarily more complicated. The requirements of "objective" cognition, factual and moral, in a racial polity are in a sense more demanding in that officially sanctioned reality is divergent from actual reality. So here, it could be said, one has an agreement to *mis*interpret the world. One has to learn to see the world wrongly, but with the assurance that this set of mistaken perceptions will be validated by white epistemic authority, whether religious or secular.

Thus in effect, on matters related to race, the Racial Contract prescribes for its signatories an inverted epistemology, an epistemology of ignorance, a particular pattern of localized and global cognitive dysfunctions (which are psychologically and socially functional), producing the ironic outcome that whites will in general be unable to understand the world they themselves have made. Part of what it means to be constructed as "white" (the metamorphosis of the sociopolitical contract), part of what it requires to achieve Whiteness, successfully to become a white person (one imagines a ceremony with certificates attending the successful rite of passage: "Congratulations, you're now an official white person!"), is a cognitive model that precludes self-transparency and genuine understanding of social realities. To a significant extent, then, white signatories will live in an invented delusional world, a racial fantasyland, a "consensual hallucination," to quote William Gibson's famous characterization of cyberspace, though this particular hallucination is located in real space.[12] There will be white mythologies, invented Orients, invented Africas, invented Americas, with a correspondingly fabricated population, countries that never were, inhabited by people who never were—Calibans and Tontos, Man Fridays and Sambos—but who attain a virtual reality through their existence in travelers' tales, folk myth, popular and highbrow fiction, colonial reports, scholarly theory, Hollywood cinema, living in the white imagination and determinedly imposed on their alarmed real-life counterparts.[13] One could say then, as a general rule, that *white misunderstanding, misrepresentation, evasion, and self-deception on matters related to race* are among the most pervasive mental phenomena of the past few hundred years, a cognitive and moral economy psychically required for conquest, colonization, and enslavement. And these phenomena are in no way *accidental*, but *prescribed* by the terms of the Racial Contract, which requires a certain schedule of structured blindnesses and opacities in order to establish and maintain the white polity.

The Racial Contract is a historical actuality.

The social contract in its modern version has long since given up any pretensions to be able to explain the historical origins of society and the state. Whereas the classic contractarians were engaged in a project both descriptive and prescriptive, the modern Rawls-inspired contract is purely a prescriptive thought experiment. And even Pateman's Sexual Contract, though its focus is the real rather than the ideal, is not meant as a literal account of what men in 4004 B.C. decided to do on the plains of Mesopotamia. Whatever accounts for what Frederick Engels once called "the *world historical defeat of the female sex*"[14]—whether the development of an economic surplus, as he theorized, or the male discovery of the capacity to rape and the female disadvantage of being the childbearing half of the species, as radical feminists have argued—it is clearly lost in antiquity.

By contrast, ironically, the Racial Contract, never so far as I know explored as such, has the best claim to being an actual historical fact. Far from being lost in the mists of the ages, it is clearly historically locatable in the series of events marking the creation of the modern world by European colonialism and the voyages of "discovery" now increasingly and more appropriately called expeditions of conquest. The Columbian quincentenary a few years ago, with its accompanying debates, polemics, controversies, counterdemonstrations, and out-pourings of revisionist literature, confronted many whites with the uncomfortable fact, hardly discussed in mainstream moral and political theory, that we live in a world which has been *foundationally shaped for the past five hundred years by the realities of European domination and the gradual con-solidation of global white supremacy.* Thus not only is the Racial Contract "real," but—whereas the social contract is characteristically taken to be establishing the legitimacy of the nation-state, and codifying morality and law within its boundaries—the Racial Contract is *global,* involving a tec-tonic shift of the ethicojuridical basis of the planet as a whole, the division of the world, as Jean-Paul Sartre put it long ago, between "men" and "natives."[15]

Europeans thereby emerge as "the lords of human kind," the "lords of all the world," with the increasing power to determine the standing of the non-Europeans who are their subjects.[16] Although no single act literally corresponds to the drawing up and signing of a contract, there is a series of acts—papal bulls and other theological pronouncements; European discussions about colonialism, "discovery," and international law; pacts, treaties, and legal decisions; academic and popular debates about the humanity of nonwhites; the establishment of formalized legal structures of differential treatment; and the routinization of informal illegal or quasi-legal practices effectively sanctioned by the complicity of silence and government failure to intervene and punish perpetrators—which collectively can be seen, not just metaphorically but close to literally, as its conceptual, juridical, and normative equivalent.

Anthony Pagden suggests that a division of the European empires into their main temporal periods should recognize "two distinct, but interdependent histories": the colonization of the Americas, 1492 to the 1830s, and the occupation of Asia, Africa, and the Pacific, 1730s to the period after World War II.[17] In the first period, it was, to begin with, the nature and moral status of the Native Americans that primarily had to be determined, and then that of the imported African slaves whose labor was required to build this "New World." In the second period, culminating in formal European colonial rule over most of the world by the early twentieth century, it was the character of colonial peoples that became crucial. But in all cases "race" is the common conceptual denominator that gradually came to signify the respective global statuses of superiority and inferiority, privilege and subordination. There is an opposition of us against them with multiple overlapping dimensions: Europeans versus non-Europeans (geography), civilized versus wild/savage/barbarians (culture), Christians versus heathens (religion). But they all eventually coalesced into the *basic* opposition of white versus nonwhite.

A Lumbee Indian legal scholar, Robert Williams, has traced the evolution of the Western legal position on the rights of native peoples from its medieval antecedents to the beginnings of the modern period, showing how it is consistently based on the assumption of "the rightness and necessity of subjugating and assimilating other peoples to [the European] worldview."[18] Initially the intellectual framework was a theological one, with normative inclusion and exclusion manifesting itself as the demarcation between Christians and heathens. The pope's powers over the *Societas Christiana,* the universal Christian commonwealth, were seen as "extending not only over all Christians within the universal commonwealth, but over unregenerated heathens and infidels as well," and this policy would subsequently underwrite not merely the Crusades against Islam but the later voyages to the Americas. Sometimes papal pronouncements did grant rights and rationality to nonbelievers. As a result of dealing with the Mongols in the thirteenth century, for example, Pope Innocent IV "conceded that infidels and heathens possessed the natural law right to elect their own secular leaders," and Pope Paul III's famous *Sublimis Deus* (1537) stated that Native Americans were rational beings, not to be treated as "dumb brutes created for our service" but "as truly men . . . capable of understanding the Catholic faith."[19] But as Williams points out, the latter qualification was always crucial. A Eurocentrically normed conception of rationality made it coextensive with acceptance of the Christian message, so that rejection was proof of bestial irrationality.

Even more remarkably, in the case of Native Americans this acceptance was to be signaled by their agreement to the *Requerimiento,* a long statement read aloud to them in, of course, a language they did not understand, failing which assent a just war could lawfully be waged against them.[20] One author writes:

> The *requerimiento* is the prototypical example of *text* justifying conquest. Informing the Indians that their lands were entrusted by Christ to the pope and thence to the kings of Spain, the document offers freedom from slavery for those Indians who accept Spanish rule. Even though it was entirely

incomprehensible to a non-Spanish speaker, reading the document provided sufficient justification for dispossession of land and immediate enslavement of the indigenous people. [Bartolomé de] Las Casas's famous comment on the *requerimiento* was that one does not know "whether to laugh or cry at the absurdity of it." . . . While appearing to respect "rights" the *requerimiento*, in fact, takes them away.[21]

In effect, then, the Catholic Church's declarations either formally legitimated conquest or could be easily circumvented where a weak prima facie moral barrier was erected.

The growth of the Enlightenment and the rise of secularism did not *challenge* this strategic dichotomization (Christian/infidel) so much as translate it into other forms. Philip Curtin refers to the characteristic "exceptionalism in European thought about the non-West," "a conception of the world largely based on self-identification—and identification of 'the other people.'"[22] Similarly, Pierre van den Berghe describes the "Enlightenment dichotomization" of the normative theories of the period.[23] "Race" gradually became the formal marker of this differentiated status, replacing the religious divide (whose disadvantage, after all, was that it could always be overcome through conversion). Thus a category crystallized over time in European thought to represent entities who are *humanoid* but not fully *human* ("savages," "barbarians") and who are identified as such by being members of the general set of nonwhite races. Influenced by the ancient Roman distinction between the civilized within and the barbarians outside the empire, the distinction between full and question-mark humans, Europeans set up a two-tiered moral code with one set of rules for whites and another for nonwhites.[24]

Correspondingly, various moral and legal doctrines were

propounded which can be seen as specific manifestations and instantiations, appropriately adjusted to circumstances, of the overarching Racial Contract. These were specific subsidiary contracts designed for different modes of exploiting the resources and peoples of the rest of the world for Europe: the expropriation contract, the slavery contract, the colonial contract.

The "Doctrine of Discovery," for example, what Williams identifies as the "paradigmatic tenet informing and determining contemporary European legal discourse respecting relations with Western tribal societies," was central to the expropriation contract.[25] The American Justice Joseph Story glossed it as granting Europeans

> an absolute dominion over the whole territories afterwards occupied by them, not in virtue of any conquest of, or cession by, the Indian natives, but as a right acquired by discovery. . . . The title of the Indians was not treated as a right of property and dominion, but as a mere right of occupancy. As infidels, heathens, and savages, they were not allowed to possess the prerogatives belonging to absolute, sovereign, and independent nations. The territory over which they wandered, and which they used for their temporary and fugitive purposes, was, in respect to Christians, deemed as if it were inhabited only by brute animals.[26]

Similarly, the slavery contract gave Europeans the right to enslave Native Americans and Africans at a time when slavery was dead or dying out in Europe, based on doctrines of the inherent inferiority of these peoples. A classic statement of the slavery contract is the 1857 *Dred Scott v. Sanford* U.S. Supreme Court decision of Chief Justice Roger Taney, which stated that blacks had for more than a century before been regarded as beings of an inferior order, and altogether unfit to associate with the white race, either in social or political relations; and so far inferior, that they had no rights which the white man was bound to respect; and that the negro might justly and lawfully be reduced to slavery for his benefit. . . . This opinion was at that time fixed and universal in the civilized portion of the white race. It was regarded as an axiom in morals as well as in politics, which no one thought of disputing, or supposed to be open to dispute.[27]

Finally, there is the colonial contract, which legitimated European rule over the nations in Asia, Africa, and the Pacific. Consider, for instance, this wonderful example, almost literally "contractarian" in character, from the French imperial theorist Jules Harmand (1845–1921), who devised the notion of *association:*

Expansion by conquest, however necessary, seems especially unjust and disturbing to the conscience of democracies. . . . But to transpose democratic institutions into such a setting is aberrant nonsense. The subject people are not and cannot become citizens in the democratic sense of the term. . . . It is necessary, then, to accept as a principle and point of departure the fact that there is a hierarchy of races and civilizations, and that we belong to the superior race and civilization. . . . The basic legitimation of conquest over native peoples is the conviction of our superiority, not merely our mechanical, economic, and military superiority, but our moral superiority. Our dignity rests on that quality, and it underlies our right to direct the rest of humanity.

What is therefore necessary is a "'Contract' of Association":

Without falling into Rousseauan reveries, it is worth noting that association implies a contract, and this idea, though nothing more than an illustration, is more appropriately applied to the coexistence of two profoundly different societies thrown sharply and artificially into contact than it is to the single society formed by natural processes which Rousseau envisaged. This is how the terms of this implicit agreement can be conceived. The European conqueror brings order, foresight, and security to a human society which, though ardently aspiring for these fundamental values without which no community can make progress, still lacks the aptitude to achieve them from within itself. . . . With these mental and material instruments, which it lacked and now receives, it gains the idea and ambition for a better existence, and the means of achieving it. We will obey you, say the subjects, if you begin by proving yourself worthy. We will obey you if you can succeed in convincing us of the superiority of that civilization of which you talk so much.[28]

Indian laws, slave codes, and colonial native acts formally codified the subordinate status of nonwhites and (ostensibly) regulated their treatment, creating a juridical space for non-Europeans as a separate category of beings. So even if there was sometimes an attempt to prevent "abuses" (and these codes were honored far more often in the breach than the observance), the point is that "abuse" as a concept presupposes as a norm the *legitimacy* of the subordination. Slavery and colonialism are not conceived as wrong in their denial of autonomy to persons; what is wrong is the improper administration of these regimes.

It would be a fundamental error, then—a point to which I will return—to see racism as anomalous, a mysterious deviation from European Enlightenment humanism. Rather, it needs to be realized that, in keeping with the Roman precedent, *European humanism usually meant that only Europeans were human.* European moral and political theory, like European thought in general, developed within the framework of the Racial Contract and, as a rule, took it for granted. As Edward Said points out in *Culture and Imperialism,* we must not see culture as "antiseptically quarantined from its worldly affiliations." But this occupational blindness has in fact infected most "professional humanists" (and certainly most philosophers), so that "as a result [they are] unable to make the connection between the prolonged and sordid cruelty of practices such as slavery, colonialist and racial oppression, and imperial subjection on the one hand, and the poetry, fiction, philosophy of the society that engages in these practices on the other."[29] By the nineteenth century, conventional white opinion casually assumed the uncontroversial validity of a hierarchy of "higher" and "lower," "master" and "subject" races, for whom, it is obvious, different rules must apply.

The modern world was thus expressly created as a *racially hierarchical* polity, globally dominated by Europeans. A 1969 *Foreign Affairs* article worth rereading today reminds us that as late as the 1940s the world "was still by and large a Western white-dominated world. The long-established patterns of white power and nonwhite non-power were still the generally accepted order of things. All the accompanying assumptions and mythologies about race and color were still mostly taken for granted. . . . [W]hite supremacy was a generally assumed and accepted state of affairs in the United States as well as in Europe's empires."[30] But statements of such frankness are rare or nonexistent in mainstream white opinion today, which generally seeks to rewrite the past so as to deny or minimize the obvious fact of global white domination.

27

Yet the United States itself, of course, is a white settler state on territory expropriated from its aborginal inhabitants through a combination of military force, disease, and a "century of dishonor" of broken treaties.[31] The expropriation involved literal genocide (a word now unfortunately devalued by hyperbolic overuse) of a kind that some recent revisionist historians have argued needs to be seen as comparable to the Third Reich's.[32] Washington, Father of the Nation, was, understandably, known somewhat differently to the Senecas as "Town Destroyer."[33] In the Declaration of Independence, Jefferson characterized Native Americans as "merciless Indian Savages," and in the Constitution, blacks, of course, appear only obliquely, through the famous "60 percent solution." Thus, as Richard Drinnon concludes: "The Framers manifestly established a government under which non-Europeans were not men created equal—in the white polity . . . they were nonpeoples."[34] Though on a smaller scale and not always so ruthlessly (or, in the case of New Zealand, because of more successful indigenous resistance), what are standardly classified as the other white settler states—for example, Canada, Australia, New Zealand, Rhodesia, and South Africa—were all founded on similar policies: the extermination, displacement, and/or herding onto reservations of the aboriginal population.[35] Pierre van den Berghe has coined the illuminating phrase *"Herrenvolk* democracies" to describe these polities, which captures perfectly the dichotomization of the Racial Contract.[36] Their subsequent evolution has been somewhat different, but defenders of South Africa's system of apartheid often argued that U.S. criticism was hypocritical in light of its own history of jim crow, especially since de facto segregation remains sufficiently entrenched that even today, forty years after *Brown v. Board of Education*, two American sociologists can title their study *American Apartheid*.[37] The racist record of preliberation Rhodesia (now Zimbabwe) and South Africa is well known; not so familiar may be the fact that the United States, Canada, and Australia all maintained "white" immigration policies until a few decades ago, and native peoples in all three countries suffer high poverty, infant mortality, and suicide rates.

Elsewhere, in Latin America, Asia, and Africa, large parts of the world were colonized, that is, formally brought under the rule of one or another of the European powers (or, later, the United States): the early Spanish and Portuguese empires in the Americas, the Philippines, and south Asia; the jealous competition from Britain, France, and Holland; the British conquest of India; the French expansion into Algeria and Indochina; the Dutch advance into Indonesia; the Opium Wars against China; the late nineteenth-century "scramble for Africa"; the U.S. war against Spain, seizure of Cuba, Puerto Rico, and the Philippines, and annexation of Hawaii.[38] The pace of change this century has been so dramatic that it is easy to forget that less than a hundred years ago, in 1914, "Europe held a grand total of roughly 85 percent of the earth as colonies, protectorates, dependencies, dominions, and commonwealths. No other associated set of colonies in history was as large, none so totally dominated, none so unequal in power to the Western metropolis."[39] One could say that the Racial Contract creates a transnational white polity, a virtual community of people linked by their citizenship in Europe at home and abroad (Europe proper, the colonial greater Europe, and the "fragments" of Euro-America, Euro-Australia, etc.), and constituted in opposition to their indigenous subjects. In most of Africa and Asia, where colonial rule ended only after World War II, rigid "color bars" maintained the separation between Europeans and indigenes. As European, as white, one knew oneself to be a member of the superior race, one's skin being one's passport: "Whatever a white man did must in some grotesque fashion be 'civilized.'"[40] So though there were local variations in the Racial Contract, depending on circumstances and the particular mode of exploitation—for example, a bipolar racial system in the (Anglo) United States, as against a subtler color hierarchy in (Iberian) Latin America—it remains the case that the white tribe, as the global representative of civilization and modernity, is generally on top of the social pyramid.[41]

We live, then, in a world built on the Racial Contract. That we do is simultaneously quite obvious if you think about it (the dates and details of colonial conquest, the constitutions of these states and their exclusionary juridical mechanisms, the histories of official racist ideologies, the battles against slavery and colonialism, the formal and informal structures of discrimination, are all within recent historical memory and, of course, massively documented in other disciplines) and nonobvious, since most whites *don't* think about it or don't think about it as the outcome of a history of political oppression but rather as just "the way things are." ("You say we're all over the world because we *conquered* the world? Why would you put it that way?") In the Treaty of Tordesillas (1494) which divided the world between Spain and Portugal, the Valladolid (Spain) Conference (1550–1551) to decide whether Native Americans were really human, the later debates over African slavery and abolitionism, the Berlin Conference (1884–1885) to partition Africa, the various inter-European pacts, treaties, and informal arrangements on policing their colonies, the post–World War I discussions in Versailles after a war to make the world safe for democracy—we see (or should see) with complete clarity a world being governed by white people. So though there is also internal conflict—disagreements, battles, even world wars—the dominant movers and shapers will be Europeans at home and abroad, with non-Europeans lining up to fight under their respective banners, and the system of white domination itself rarely being challenged. (The exception, of course, is Japan, which escaped colonization, and so for most of the twentieth century has had a shifting and ambivalent relationship with the global white polity.) The legacy of this world is, of course, still with us today, in the economic, political, and cultural domination of the planet by Europeans and their descendants. The fact that this racial structure, clearly political in character, and the struggle against it, equally so, have *not* for the most part been deemed appropriate subject matter for mainstream Anglo-American political philosophy and the fact that the very concepts hegemonic in the discipline are refractory to an understanding of these realities, reveal at best, a disturbing provincialism and an ahistoricity profoundly at odds with the radically foundational questioning on which philosophy prides itself and, at worst, a complicity with the terms of the Racial Contract itself.

The Racial Contract is an exploitation contract that creates global European economic domination and national white racial privilege.

The classic social contract, as I have detailed, is primarily moral/political in nature. But it is also *economic* in the background sense that the point of leaving the state of nature is in part to secure a stable environment for the industrious appropriation of the world. (After all, one famous definition of politics is that it is about who gets what and why.) Thus even in Locke's moralized state of nature, where people generally do obey natural law, he is concerned about the safety of private property, indeed proclaiming that "the great and *chief end* therefore, of Mens uniting into Commonwealths, and putting themselves under Government, *is the Preservation of their*

31

Property."[42] And in Hobbes's famously amoral and unsafe state of nature, we are told that "there is no place for Industry; because the fruit thereof is uncertain; and consequently no Culture of the Earth."[43] So part of the point of bringing society into existence, with its laws and enforcers of the law, is to protect what you have accumulated.

What, then, is the nature of the economic system of the new society? The general contract does not itself prescribe a particular model or particular schedule of property rights, requiring only that the "equality" in the prepolitical state be somehow preserved. This provision may be variously interpreted as a self-interested surrender to an absolutist Hobbesian government that itself determines property rights, or a Lockean insistence that private property accumulated in the moralized state of nature be respected by the constitutionalist government. Or more radical political theorists, such as socialists and feminists, might argue that state-of-nature equality actually mandates class or gender economic egalitarianism in society. So, different political interpretations of the initial moral egalitarianism can be advanced, but the general background idea is that the equality of human beings in the state of nature is somehow (whether as equality of opportunity or as equality of outcome) supposed to carry over into the economy of the created sociopolitical order, leading to a system of voluntary human intercourse and exchange in which exploitation is precluded.

By contrast, the economic dimension of the Racial Contract is the *most* salient, foreground rather than background, since the Racial Contract is calculatedly aimed at economic exploitation. The whole point of establishing a moral hierarchy and juridically partitioning the polity according to race is to secure and legitimate the privileging of those individuals designated as white/persons and the exploitation of those individuals designated as nonwhite/subpersons. There are other benefits accruing from the Racial Contract—far greater political influence, cultural hegemony, the psychic payoff that comes from knowing one is a member of the *Herrenvolk* (what W. E. B. Du Bois once called "the wages of whiteness")[44]—but the bottom line is material advantage. Globally, the Racial Contract creates Europe as the continent that dominates the world; locally, within Europe and the other continents, it designates Europeans as the privileged race.

The challenge of explaining what has been called "the European miracle"—the rise of Europe to global domination—has long exercised both academic and lay opinion.[45] How is it that a formerly peripheral region on the outskirts of the Asian land mass, at the far edge of the trade routes, remote from the great civilizations of Islam and the East, was able in a century or two to achieve global political and economic dominance? The explanations historically given by Europeans themselves have varied tremendously, from the straightforwardly racist and geographically determinist to the more subtly environmentalist and culturalist. But what they have all had in common, even those influenced by Marxism, is their tendency to depict this development as essentially autochthonous, their tendency to privilege some set of internal variables and correspondingly downplay or ignore altogether the role of colonial conquest and African slavery. Europe made it on its own, it is said, because of the peculiar characteristics of Europe and Europeans.

Thus whereas no reputable historian today would espouse the frankly biologistic theories of the past, which made Europeans (in both pre- and post-Darwinian accounts) inherently the most advanced race, as contrasted with the backward/less-evolved races elsewhere, the thesis of European specialness and exceptionalism is still presupposed. It is still assumed that rationalism and science, innovativeness and inventiveness found their special home here, as against the intellectual stagnation and traditionalism of the rest of the world, so that Europe was therefore destined in advance to occupy the special position in global history it has. James Blaut calls this the theory, or "super-theory" (an umbrella covering many different versions: theological, cultural, biologistic, geographical, technological, etc.), of "Eurocentric diffusionism," according to which European progress is seen as "natural" and asymmetrically determinant of the fate of non-Europe.[46] Similarly, Sandra Harding, in her anthology on the "racial" economy of science, cites "the assumption that Europe functions autonomously from other parts of the world; that Europe is its own origin, final end, and agent; and that Europe and people of European descent in the Americas and elsewhere owe nothing to the rest of the world."[47]

Unsurprisingly, black and Third World theorists have traditionally dissented from this notion of happy divine or natural European dispensation. They have claimed, quite to the contrary, that there is a crucial causal connection between European advance and the unhappy fate of the rest of the world. One classic example of such scholarship from a half century ago was the Caribbean historian Eric Williams's *Capitalism and Slavery*, which argued that the profits from African slavery helped to make the industrial revolution possible, so that internalist accounts were fundamentally mistaken.[48] And in recent years, with decolonization, the rise of the New Left in the United States, and the entry of more alternative voices into the academy, this challenge has deepened and broadened. There are variations in the authors' positions—for example, Walter Rodney, Samir Amin, André Gunder Frank, Immanuel Wallerstein[49]—but the basic theme is that the exploitation of the empire (the bullion from the great gold and silver mines

34

in Mexico and Peru, the profits from plantation slavery, the fortunes made by the colonial companies, the general social and economic stimulus provided by the opening up of the "New World") was to a greater or lesser extent crucial in enabling and then consolidating the takeoff of what had previously been an economic backwater. It was far from the case that Europe was specially destined to assume economic hegemony; there were a number of centers in Asia and Africa of a comparable level of development which could potentially have evolved in the same way. But the European ascent closed off this development path for others because it forcibly inserted them into a colonial network whose exploitative relations and extractive mechanisms prevented autonomous growth.

Overall, then, colonialism "lies at the heart" of the rise of Europe.[50] The economic unit of analysis needs to be Europe as a whole, since it is not always the case that the colonizing nations directly involved always benefited in the long term. Imperial Spain, for example, still feudal in character, suffered massive inflation from its bullion imports. But through trade and financial exchange, others launched on the capitalist path, such as Holland, profited. Internal national rivalries continued, of course, but this common identity based on the transcontinental exploitation of the non-European world would in many cases be politically crucial, generating a sense of Europe as a cosmopolitan entity engaged in a common enterprise, underwritten by race. As Victor Kiernan puts it, "All countries within the European orbit benefited however, as Adam Smith pointed out, from colonial contributions to a common stock of wealth, bitterly as they might wrangle over ownership of one territory or another. . . . [T]here was a sense in which all Europeans shared in a heightened sense of power engendered by the successes of any of them, as well as in the pool of material wealth . . . that the colonies produced."[51]

Today, correspondingly, though formal decolonization has taken place and in Africa and Asia black, brown, and yellow natives are in office, ruling independent nations, the global economy is essentially dominated by the former colonial powers, their offshoots (Euro–United States, Euro-Canada), and their international financial institutions, lending agencies, and corporations. (As previously observed, the notable exception, whose history confirms rather than challenges the rule, is Japan, which escaped colonization and, after the Meiji Restoration, successfully embarked on its own industrialization.) Thus one could say that the world is essentially dominated by white capital. Global figures on income and property ownership are, of course, broken down nationally rather than racially, but if a transnational racial disaggregation were to be done, it would reveal that whites control a percentage of the world's wealth grossly disproportionate to their numbers. Since there is no reason to think that the chasm between First and Third Worlds (which largely coincides with this racial division) is going to be bridged—vide the abject failure of various United Nations plans from the "development decade" of the 1960s onward—it seems undeniable that for years to come, the planet will be white dominated. With the collapse of communism and the defeat of Third World attempts to seek alternative paths, the West reigns supreme, as celebrated in a London *Financial Times* headline: "The fall of the Soviet bloc has left the IMF and G7 to rule the world and create a new imperial age."[52] Economic structures have been set in place, causal processes established, whose outcome is to pump wealth from one side of the globe to another, and which will continue to work largely independently of the ill will/good will, racist/ antiracist feelings of particular individuals. This globally color-coded distribution of wealth and poverty has been produced by the Racial Contract and in turn reinforces adherence to it in its signatories and beneficiaries.

Moreover, it is not merely that Europe and the former white settler states are globally dominant but that *within* them, where there is a significant nonwhite presence (indigenous peoples, descendants of imported slaves, voluntary nonwhite immigration), whites continue to be privileged vis-à-vis nonwhites. The old structures of formal, de jure exclusion have largely been dismantled, the old explicitly biologistic ideologies largely abandoned[53]—the Racial Contract, as will be discussed later, is continually being rewritten—but opportunities for nonwhites, though they have expanded, remain below those for whites. The claim is not, of course, that all whites are better off than all nonwhites, but that, as a statistical generalization, the objective life chances of whites are significantly better.

As an example, consider the United States. A series of books has recently documented the decline of the integrationist hopes raised by the 1960s and the growing intransigence and hostility of whites who think they have "done enough," despite the fact that the country continues to be massively segregated, median black family incomes have begun falling by comparison to white family incomes after some earlier closing of the gap, the so-called "black underclass" has basically been written off, and reparations for slavery and post-Emancipation discrimination have never been paid, or, indeed, even seriously considered.[54] Recent work on racial inequality by Melvin Oliver and Thomas Shapiro suggests that wealth is more important than income in determining the likelihood of future racial equalization, since it has a cumulative effect that is passed down through intergenerational transfer, affecting life chances and opportunities for one's children. Whereas in 1988 black households earned sixty-two cents for every dollar earned by white households, the comparative differential with regard to wealth is much greater and, arguably, provides a more realistically negative picture of the prospects for closing the racial gap: "Whites possess nearly twelve times as much median net worth as blacks, or $43,800 versus $3,700. In an even starker contrast, perhaps, the average white household controls $6,999 in net financial assets while the average black household retains no NFA nest egg whatsoever." Moreover, the analytic focus on wealth rather than income exposes how illusory the much-trumpeted rise of a "black middle class" is: "Middle-class blacks, for example, earn seventy cents for every dollar earned by middle-class whites but they possess only fifteen cents for every dollar of wealth held by middle-class whites." This huge disparity in white and black wealth is not remotely contingent, accidental, fortuitous; it is the direct outcome of American state policy and the collusion with it of the white citizenry. In effect, "materially, whites and blacks constitute two nations,"[55] the white nation being constituted by the American Racial Contract in a relationship of structured racial exploitation with the black (and, of course, historically also the red) nation.

A collection of papers from panels organized in the 1980s by the National Economic Association, the professional organization of black economists, provides some insight into the mechanics and the magnitude of such exploitative transfers and denials of opportunity to accumulate material and human capital. It takes as its title *The Wealth of Races*—an ironic tribute to Adam Smith's famous book *The Wealth of Nations*— and analyzes the different varieties of discrimination to which blacks have been subjected: slavery, employment discrimination, wage discrimination, promotion discrimination, white monopoly power discrimination against black capital, racial price discrimination in consumer goods, housing, services, insurance, etc.[56] Many of these, by their very nature, are difficult to quantify; moreover, there are costs in anguish and suffering that can never really be compensated. Nonetheless, those that do lend themselves to calculation offer some remarkable figures. (The figures are unfortunately dated; readers should multiply by a factor that takes fifteen years of inflation into account.) If one were to do a calculation of the *cumulative* benefits (through compound interest) from labor market discrimination over the forty-year period from 1929 to 1969 and adjust for inflation, then in 1983 dollars, the figure would be over $1.6 trillion.[57] An estimate for the total of "diverted income" from slavery, 1790 to 1860, compounded and translated into 1983 dollars, would yield the sum of $2.1 trillion to $4.7 trillion.[58] And if one were to try to work out the cumulative value, with compound interest, of unpaid slave labor before 1863, underpayment. since 1863, and denial of opportunity to acquire land and natural resources available to white settlers, then the total amount required to compensate blacks "could take more than the entire wealth of the United States."[59]

So this gives an idea of the centrality of racial exploitation to the U.S. economy and the dimensions of the payoff for its white beneficiaries from one nation's Racial Contract. But this very centrality, these very dimensions render the topic taboo, virtually undiscussed in the debates on justice of most white political theory. If there is such a backlash against affirmative action, what would the response be to the demand for the interest on the unpaid forty acres and a mule? These issues cannot be raised because they go to the heart of the real nature of the polity and its structuring by the Racial Contract. White moral theory's debates on justice in the state must therefore inevitably have a somewhat farcical air, since they ignore the central injustice on which the state rests. (No won-der a hypothetical contractarianism that evades the actual circumstances of the polity's founding is preferred!)

Both globally and within particular nations, then, white people, Europeans and their descendants, continue to benefit from the Racial Contract, which creates a world in their cultural image, political states differentially favoring their interests, an economy structured around the racial exploitation of others, and a moral psychology (not just in whites but sometimes in nonwhites also) skewed consciously or unconsciously toward privileging them, taking the status quo of differential racial entitlement as normatively legitimate, and not to be investigated further.

DETAILS

So that gives us the overview. Let us now move to a closer examination of the details and workings of the Racial Contract: its norming of space and the (sub)person, its relation to the "official" social contract, and the terms of its enforcement.

The Racial Contract norms (and races) space, demarcating civil and wild spaces.

Neither space nor the individual is usually an object of explicit and detailed norming for the mainstream social contract. Space is just *there*, taken for granted, and the individual is tacitly posited as the white adult male, so that all individuals are obviously equal. But for the Racial Contract, space itself and the individuals therein are not homogeneous; so explicit normative distinctions necessarily have to be made. I will treat the norming of space and the person separately, though exegesis is complicated by the fact that they are bound up together. The norming of space is partially done in terms of the *racing* of space, the depiction of space as dominated by individuals (whether persons or subpersons) of a certain race. At the same time, the norming of the individual is partially achieved by *spacing* it, that is, representing it as imprinted with the characteristics of a certain kind of space. So this is a mutually supporting characterization that, for subpersons, becomes a circular indictment: "You are what you are in part because you originate from a certain kind of space, and that space has those properties in part because it is inhabited by creatures like yourself."

The supposedly abstract but actually white social contract characterizes (European) space basically as presociopolitical ("the state of nature") and postsociopolitical (the locus of "civil society"). But this characterization does not reflect negatively on the characteristics of the space itself or its denizens. This space is *our* space, a space in which we (we white people) are at home, a cozy domestic space. At a certain stage, (white) people seeing the disadvantages of the state of nature voluntarily choose to leave it, thenceforth establishing institutions transforming its character. But there is nothing *innate* in the space or the persons that connotes intrinsic defect.

By contrast, in the social contract's application to non-Europe, where it becomes the Racial Contract, both space and its inhabitants are alien. So this space and these individuals need to be explicitly theorized about, since (it turns out) they are both defective in a way that requires external intervention to be redeemed (insofar, that is, as redemption is possible). Europeans, or at least full Europeans, were "civilized," and this condition was manifested in the character of the spaces they inhabited.[1] Non-Europeans were "savages," and this condition was manifested in the character of the spaces *they* inhabited. In fact, as has been pointed out, this habitation is captured in the etymology of "savage" itself, which derives from the Latin *silva*, "wood," so that the savage is the wild man of the wood, *silvaticus, homo sylvestris,* the man into whose being wildness, wilderness, has so deeply penetrated that the door to civilization, to the political, is barred.[2] (You can take the Wild Man out of the wilderness, but you can't take the wilderness out of the Wild Man.) The Wild Man is a crucial figure in medieval thought, the domestic antipode (*within* Europe) of civilization, and is one of the conceptual antecedents of the later *extra*-European "savages."[3] As Hayden White points out, the creation of the "Wild Man" illustrates "the technique of ostensive self-definition by negation,"[4] the characterization of oneself by reference to what one is not. Who are we? We are the nonsavages. Thus it is really here, in the real-life Racial Contract, as against the mythical social contract, that the "state of nature" and the "natural" play their decisive theoretical role. *They* are in the state of nature, and *we* are not. Englishmen, writes Roy Harvey Pearce, "found in America not only an uncivilized environment, but uncivilized men—natural men, as it was said, living in a natural world."[5]

Correspondingly, the Racial Contract in its early preconquest versions must necessarily involve the pejorative characterization of the spaces that need taming, the spaces in which the racial polities are eventually going to be constructed. The Racial Contract is thus necessarily more openly *material* than the social contract. These strange landscapes (so unlike those at home), this alien flesh (so different from our own), must be mapped and subordinated. Creating the civil and the political here thus requires an active *spatial* struggle (this space is resistant) against the savage and barbaric, an advancing of the frontier against opposition, a Europeanization of the world. "Europe," as Mary Louise Pratt notes, "came to see itself as a 'planetary process' rather than simply a region of the world."[6] Space must be normed and raced at the *macro*level (entire countries and continents), the *local* level (city neighborhoods), and ultimately even the *micro*level of the body itself (the contaminated and contaminating carnal halo of the non-white body).

There are two main dimensions to this norming: the epistemological and the moral.

The epistemological dimension is the corollary of the preemptive restriction of knowledge to European cognizers, which implies that in certain spaces real knowledge (knowledge of science, universals) is not possible. Significant cultural achievement, intellectual progress, is thus denied to those spaces, which are deemed (failing European intervention) to be permanently locked into a cognitive state of superstition and ignorance. Valentin Mudimbe refers to this as an "epistemological ethnocentrism." Countervailing evidence may then be treated in different ways. It may simply be destroyed, as for example the invading Spanish conquistadors burned Aztec manuscripts. It may be explained away as resulting from the intervention of outsiders, for example from a previously unknown contact with whites: "Since Africans could produce nothing of value; the technique of Yoruba statuary must have come from Egyptians; Benin art must be a Portuguese creation; the architectural achievement of Zimbabwe was due to Arab technicians; and Hausa and Buganda statecraft were inventions of white invaders."[7] (Think of that favorite of comics, adventure novels, B-movies—the lost white tribe whose legacy is discovered in some faraway, otherwise benighted place on the earth, and which is responsible for whatever culture the hapless nonwhite natives may possess.) Sometimes even an extraterrestrial origin may be sought, as the desert drawings in South America have been attributed to alien visitors. Similarly, independently of the eventual outcome of the controversy recently stimulated by the claim of Martin Bernal's *Black*

Athena that ancient Egypt was a significant cultural influence on ancient Greece, and that it was to a large extent a black civilization, one can surely infer that at least *some* of the resistance to the idea in establishment white scholarship comes from the aprioristic presumption that no such achievement could really have come from black (and ultimately "sub-Saharan") Africa.[8] (The phrase "sub-Saharan Africa" is itself, in fact, a geographic marker motivated by the Racial Contract.) Finally, the cultural achievements of others may simply be appropriated by Europe without acknowledgment, in effect denying the reality that "'the West' has always been a multicultural creation."[9]

This norming is, of course, also manifested in the vocabulary of "discovery" and "exploration" still in use until recently, basically implying that if no white person has been there before, then cognition cannot really have taken place. In *Heart of Darkness*, Joseph Conrad's Marlow pores over the globe and notes that "there were many blank spaces on the earth."[10] And this blankness signifies not merely that Europeans have not arrived but that these *spaces* have not arrived, a blankness of the inhabitants themselves. Africa is thus the "Dark Continent" because of the paucity of (remembered) European contact with it. Correspondingly, there are rituals of naming which serve to seize the terrain of these "New" Worlds and incorporate them into *our* world: New England, New Holland, New France—in a word, "New Europes," "cultural-spatial extension[s] of Europe."[11] They are domesticated, transformed, made familiar, made a part of our space, brought into the world of European (which is human) cognition, so they can be knowable and known. Knowledge, science, and the ability to apprehend the world intellectually are thus restricted to Europe, which emerges as *the global locus of rationality*, at least for the European cognitive agent, who will be the one to validate local knowledge claims. In order for these spaces to be known, European perception is required.

Morally, vice and virtue are *spatialized*, first on the macrolevel of a moral cartography that accompanies the literal European mapping of the world, so that entire regions, countries, indeed continents, are invested with moral qualities. Thus Mudimbe describes the "geography of monstrosity" of early European cartography, which, in a framework still largely theological, partitions the known world and points out Where There Be Dragons.[12] Non-European space is thus demonized in a way that implies the need for Europeanization if moral redemption is to be possible. The link between the cognitive and the moral, of course, connects the failure to perceive natural law with moral flaw: the darkness of the Dark Continent is not merely the absence of a European presence but a blindness to Christian light, which necessarily results in moral blackness, superstition, devil worship. Appropriately, then, one of the medieval cartographic traditions was the *mappamundi*, the map of the world organized not on a grid system, but around the Christian cross, with Jerusalem at the center.[13] Similarly, European settlers in America described the area beyond the mountains as "Indian country," "the Dark and Bloody Ground . . . a howling wilderness inhabited by 'savages and wild beasts,'" or sometimes even "Sodom and Gomorrah." And the society they saw themselves founding was, correspondingly, sometimes referred to as "New Canaan."[14]

The non-European state of nature is thus *actual*, a wild and racialized place that was originally characterized as cursed with a theological blight as well, an unholy land. The European state of nature, by contrast, is either hypothetical or, if actual, generally a tamer affair, a kind of garden gone to seed, which may need some clipping but is really *already* partially domesticated and just requires a few modifications to be appropriately transformed—a testimony to the superior moral characteristics of *this* space and its inhabitants. (Hobbes's paradigmatically ferocious state of nature may appear to be an exception, but as we will see later, it is really only literal for *non-Europeans*, so that it actually confirms rather than challenges the rule.)

Because of this moralization of space, *the journey upriver* or in general *the journey into the interior* in imperial literature—the trip away from the outposts of civilization into native territory—acquires deep symbolic significance, for it is the expedition into both the geographic and the personal heart of darkness, the evil without which correlates with the evil within. Thus in *Apocalypse Now*, Francis Ford Coppola's 1979 rewriting of Conrad in the context of Vietnam, Willard's (Martin Sheen) journey upriver to find Kurtz (Marlon Brando), whose stages are sartorially marked through the gradual stripping away of the (civilized) uniform of the U.S. army to the final mud-caked, machete-carrying figure indistinguishable from the Cambodian villagers ceremonially killing the buffalo, is both a normative *descent* into moral corruption and a cognitive *ascent* to the realization that the war could have been won only by abandoning the restraints of Euro-American civilization (as demonstrated in My Lai presumably) and embracing the "savagery" of the North Vietnamese army.[15]

The battle against this savagery is in a sense permanent as long as the savages continue to exist, contaminating (and being contaminated by) the non-Europeanized space around them. So it is not merely that space is normatively characterized on the macrolevel *before* conquest and colonial settlement, but that even *afterward*, on the local level, there are divisions, the European city and the Native Quarter, Whitetown and Niggertown/Darktown, suburb and inner city. David Theo Goldberg comments, "Power in the polis, and this is especially

true of racialized power, reflects and refines the spatial relations of its inhabitants."[16] Part of the purpose of the color bar/
the color line/apartheid/jim crow is to maintain these spaces
in their place, to have the checkerboard of virtue and vice,
light and dark space, *ours* and *theirs*, clearly demarcated so
that the human geography prescribed by the Racial Contract
can be preserved. For here the moral topography is different and
the civilizing mission as yet incomplete. Of this partitioning of
space and person, Frantz Fanon writes: "The colonial world
is a world cut in two. . . . The settlers' town is a town of white
people, of foreigners. . . . [The native town] is a town of niggers
and dirty Arabs. . . . This world divided into compartments,
this world cut in two is inhabited by two different species."[17]
In fact, the intimacy of the connection between place and
(sub)person means that perhaps it never *will* be complete, that
those associated with the jungle will take the jungle with them
even when they are brought to more civilized regions. (The
jungle is, so to speak, always waiting to reassert itself: every
évolué stands in danger of devolution.) One might argue that
in the United States the growing postwar popularity of the
locution of "urban jungle" reflects a subtextual (and not very
sub-) reference to the increasing nonwhiteness of the residents
of the inner cities, and the corresponding pattern of "white
flight" to suburban vanilla sanctuary: our space/home space/
civilized space. In America, South Africa, and elsewhere, the
white space is patrolled for dark intruders, whose very presence, independently of what they may or may not do, is a
blot on the reassuring civilized whiteness of the home space.
Consider the curfew laws in segregated neighborhoods earlier
in U.S. history (and arguably the continuing informal police
practices now), the notices that used to be posted outside
"sundown" towns—"Nigger, don't let the sun set on you

48

here!" The Racial Contract demarcates space, reserving privileged spaces for its first-class citizens.

The other dimension of moral appraisal and norming, which is of course the one that becomes more central with secularization, is not traditional Christian vice and virtue but the emergent capitalist/Protestant ethic of settlement and industry. Franke Wilmer argues that the ideology of "progress and modernization" has served for five hundred years as the dominant justification of Western displacement and killing of the "Fourth World" of indigenous peoples.[18] Here, space is nationally characterized with respect to a European standard of agriculture and industry in such a way as to render it morally open for seizure, expropriation, settlement, development— in a word, *peopling*. In the white settler states, space will sometimes be represented as literally empty and unoccupied, void, wasteland, "virgin" territory. There is just no one there. Or even if it is conceded that humanoid entities are present, it is denied that any real appropriation, any human shaping of the world, is taking place. So there is still no one there: the land is *terra nullius, vacuum domicilium*, again "virgin." "Thus in the beginning," Locke tells us, "all the World was *America.*"[19] The central and mutually complementary myths, as Francis Jennings points out, are the twin ideas of "virgin lands and savage peoples."[20] In both cases, then, this will be *unpeopled* land, inhabited at most by "varmints," "critters," "human beasts," who are an obstacle to development, rather than capable of development themselves, and whose extermination or at least clearing away is a prerequisite for civilization. A numbers game is played, involving the systematic undercounting of the aboriginal population, often by a factor of ten or more, since by definition "large populations are impossible in savage societies."[21] (And when they are no longer large, one will not want to admit how large they once were.) Richard

Drinnon describes how many European settlers in the United States thought of themselves as "inland Crusoes" in an "unpeopled" wilderness, characterized by Theodore Roosevelt as "the red wastes where the barbarian peoples of the world hold sway."[22] Similarly, "At the time of first settlement in the Australian colonies all lands were deemed to be waste lands and the property of the Crown."[23] In South Africa, the *trekboers* went on exterminatory hunting expeditions and subsequently "bragged about their bag of Bushmen as fishermen boast about their catch."[24] So the basic sequence ran something like this: there are no people there in the first place; in the second place, they're not improving the land; and in the third place—oops!— they're already all dead anyway (and, honestly, there really weren't that many to begin with), so there are no people there, as we said in the first place.

Since the Racial Contract links space with race and race with personhood, the white raced space of the polity is in a sense the geographical locus of the polity proper. Where indigenous peoples were permitted to survive, they were denied full or any membership in the political community, thus becoming foreigners in their own country. Drinnon describes this remarkable final Melvillean political confidence trick: "The country was full of recent arrivals from the East, mysterious impostors pretending to be natives and denying real natives their humanity."[25] Similarly, an Australian historian could write in 1961: "Before the Gold Rush there were, after all, few foreigners of any one race in Australia—except for the Aborigines, if we may, sheepishly I hope, call them foreigners after a manner of speaking."[26] (Where did you guys come from, anyway? You're not from around here, are you?) This raced space will also mark the geographic boundary of the state's full obligations. On the local level of spatialization, norming then manifests itself in the presumption that certain spaces (e.g., those of the inner city) are intrinsically doomed to welfare dependency, high street crime, underclass status, because of the characteristics of its inhabitants, so that the larger economic system has no role in creating these problems. Thus one of the interesting consequences of the Racial Contract is that the *political space* of the polity is not coextensive with its *geographical space*. In entering these (dark) spaces, one is entering a region normatively discontinuous with white political space, where the rules are different in ways ranging from differential funding (school resources, garbage collection, infrastructural repair) to the absence of police protection.

Finally, there is the microspace of the body itself (which in a sense is the foundation of all the other levels), the fact, to be dealt with in greater detail later, that the persons and subpersons, the citizens and noncitizens, who inhabit these polities do so embodied in envelopes of skin, flesh, hair. The nonwhite body carries a halo of blackness around it which may actually make some whites physically uncomfortable. (A black American architect of the nineteenth century trained himself to read architectural blueprints upside-down because he knew white clients would be made uncomfortable by having him on the same side of the desk as themselves.) Part of this feeling is sexual: the black body in particular is seen as paradigmatically *a body*.[27] Lewis Gordon suggests that the black "presence is a form of absence. . . . Every black person becomes a limb of an enormous black body: THE BLACK BODY."[28] Whites may get to be "talking heads," but even when blacks' heads are talking, one is always uncomfortably aware of the bodies to which these heads are attached. (So blacks are at best "talking bodies.") Early rock and roll was viewed by some white conservatives as a communist plot because it brought the rhythms of the black body into the white bodily space; it began the funky subversion of that space. These are, literally, *jungle* rhythms, telegraphed from the space of savagery, threatening the civilized space of the white polity and the carnal integrity of its inhabitants. So when in the 1950s white artists did cover versions of "race records," songs on the jim-crowed rhythm and blues charts, they were sanitized, cleaned up, the rhythms rearranged; they were made recognizably "white."

More generally, there is also the basic social requirement of distinguishing on the level of everyday interaction (an interaction taking place not on some abstract plane but *within* this racialized space) person-person from person-subperson social intercourse. Thus in the United States, from the epoch of slavery and jim crow to the modern period of formal liberty but continuing racism, the physical interactions between whites and blacks are carefully regulated by a shifting racial etiquette that is ultimately determined by the current form of the Racial Contract. In her study of how white women's lives are shaped by race, Ruth Frankenberg describes the resulting "racial social geography," the personal "boundary maintenance" that required that one "always maintained a separateness," a self-conscious "boundary demarcation of physical space."[29] Conceptions of one's white self map a micro-geography of the acceptable routes through racial space of one's own personal space. These traversals of space are imprinted with domination: prescribed postures of deference and submission for the black Other, the body language of nonuppitiness (no "reckless eyeballing"); traffic-codes of priority ("my space can walk through yours and you must step aside"); unwritten rules for determining when to acknowledge the nonwhite presence and when not, dictating spaces of intimacy and distance, zones of comfort and discomfort ("thus far and no farther"); and finally, of course, antimiscegenation laws and lynching to proscribe and punish the ultimate violation, the penetration of black into white space.[30] If, as I earlier argued, there is a sense in which the *real* polity is the virtual white polity, then, without pushing the metaphor too far, one could say that the nonwhite body is a moving bubble of wilderness in white political space, a node of discontinuity which is necessarily in permanent tension with it.

The Racial Contract norms (and races) the individual, establishing personhood and subpersonhood.

In the disincarnate political theory of the orthodox social contract, the body vanishes, becomes theoretically unimportant, just as the physical space inhabited by that body is ostensibly theoretically unimportant. But this disappearing act is just as much an illusion in the former as in the latter case. The reality is that one can pretend the body does not matter only because a particular body (the white male body) is being presupposed as the somatic norm. In a political dialogue between the owners of such bodies, the details of their flesh do not matter since they are judged to be equally rational, equally capable of perceiving natural law or their own self-interest. But as feminist theorists have pointed out, the body is only irrelevant when it's the (white) male body. Even for Kant, who defines "persons" simply as rational beings, without any apparent restrictions of gender or race, the female body demarcates one as insufficiently rational to be politically anything more than a "passive" citizen.[31] Similarly, the Racial Contract is explicitly predicated on a politics of the body which is related to the body politic through restrictions on which bodies are "politic." There are bodies impolitic whose owners are judged incapable of *forming* or fully *entering into* a body politic.

The distant intellectual antecedent here, of course, is Aristotle, who, in *The Politics* talks about "natural slaves," who need to be distinguished from those whose enslavement is merely contingent, a result, say, of being captured in battle.[32] But writing in the epoch of the *non*racial slavery of antiquity, Aristotle faced an identification problem in picking out these unfortunates. The Racial Contract basically seeks to remedy this deficiency, establishing a (relatively) clearcut line of somatic demarcation between possessors of servile and nonservile souls. As earlier mentioned, the older distinction between Europeans and non-Europeans is essentially a theological one, developed in large part through the wars in the East and South against Islam, (black) paynim both anti-Christ and anti-Europe. For the politicoeconomic project of conquest, expropriation, and settlement, this categorization has the disadvantage of being contingent. People can always convert, and if the schedule of rights is religiously based, it then becomes at least a prima facie problem (though not an insuperable one) to treat fellow Christians the way one can treat heathens. In the *City of God*, as Hayden White glosses Augustine, "even the most monstrous of men were still *men*," "salvageable in principle," "potentially capable" of being redeemed by Christian grace.[33] The new secular category of *race*, by contrast, which gradually crystallized over a century or so, had the virtue of permanency over any given individual's lifetime. Drawing on the medieval legacy of the Wild Man, and giving this a color, the Racial Contract establishes a particular somatotype as the norm, deviation from which *unfits* one for full personhood and full membership in the polity. If one is not always a natural slave, one is at least always a natural non- or second-class citizen. "In the gradual transition from religious conceptions to racial conceptions," Jennings notes, "the gulf between persons calling themselves Christian and the other persons, whom they called heathen, translated smoothly into

a chasm between whites and coloreds. The law of moral obliga-
tion sanctioned behavior on only one side of that chasm."[34]

Philosophically, one could distinguish moral/legal, cognitive, and aesthetic dimensions of this racial norming.[35]

Morally and legally, as I stated at the beginning, the Racial
Contract establishes a fundamental partition in the social ontology of the planet, which could be represented as the divide
between persons and subpersons, *Untermenschen*. "Personhood" has received a great deal of philosophical attention
in recent years because of the revival in Kantian and natural
rights moral/political theories and the relative decline of utilitarianism. Utilitarianism puts morality on the straightforward
basis of promoting social welfare: the greatest good for the
greatest number. But it is vulnerable to the charge that it
would permit the violation of the rights of some if overall
social welfare were thereby maximized. By contrast, Kantian
and natural rights theories emphasize the sanctity of individual "persons," whose rights must not be infringed even if
overall welfare would be increased.

Ideally, then, we want a world where all humans are treated
as "persons." So the notion of a "person" becomes central to
normative theory. The simplified social ontology implied by
the notion of "personhood" is itself, of course, a product of
capitalism and the eighteenth-century bourgeois revolutions.
Moses Finley points out that "inequality before the law" was
typical of the ancient world,[36] and medieval feudalism had its
own social hierarchy. Kantian personhood emerged in part
in *opposition* to this world of rank and ascribed status. The
hierarchically differentiated human values of plebeian and pa-
trician, of serf, monk, and knight, were replaced by the "infinite value" of all human beings. It is a noble and inspiring
ideal, even if its incorporation into countless manifestos, declarations, constitutions, and introductory ethics texts has now

reduced it to a homily, deprived it of the shattering political force it once had. But what needs to be emphasized is that it is only *white persons* (and really only white males) who have been able to take this for granted, for whom it can be an unexciting truism. As Lucius Outlaw underlines, European liberalism restricts "egalitarianism to equality among equals," and blacks and others are ontologically excluded by race from the promise of "the liberal project of modernity."[37] The terms of the Racial Contract mean that *nonwhite subpersonhood is enshrined simultaneously with white personhood.*

So in order to understand the workings of the polities structured by the Racial Contract, I believe, we need to understand *sub*personhood also. Subpersons are humanoid entities who, because of racial phenotype/genealogy/culture, are not fully human and therefore have a different and inferior schedule of rights and liberties applying to them. In other words, it is possible to get away with doing things to subpersons that one could not do to persons, because they do not have the same rights as persons. Insofar as racism is addressed at all within mainstream moral and political philosophy, it is usually treated in a footnote as a regrettable deviation from the ideal. But treating it this way makes it seem contingent, accidental, residual, removes it from our understanding. Race is made to seem marginal when in fact race has been central. The notion of subpersonhood, by contrast, makes the Racial Contract explicit, showing that to characterize things in terms of "deviations" is in a sense misleading. Rather, what is involved is compliance with a *norm* whose existence it is now embarrassing to admit. So instead of pretending that the social contract outlines the ideal that people tried to live up to but which they occasionally (as with all ideals) fell short of, we should say frankly that for whites the Racial Contract represented the *ideal*, and what is involved is not deviation from the (fictive) norm but *adherence* to the actual norm. (Thus, I pointed out earlier "exceptionalism" *was* the rule.) The "Racial Contract" as a theory puts race where it belongs—at center stage—and demonstrates how the polity was in fact a racial one, a white-supremacist state, for which differential white racial entitlement and nonwhite racial subordination were defining, thus inevitably molding white moral psychology and moral theorizing.

This is most clearly the case, of course, for blacks, the degradation of *racial* slavery meaning, as has often been pointed out, that for the first time (and unlike the slavery of ancient Greece and Rome or the medieval Mediterranean) *slavery acquired a color.* But for the colonial project in general, personhood would be raced, hence the concept of "subject races." The crucial conceptual divide is between whites and nonwhites, persons and subpersons, though once this central cut has been made, other internal distinctions are possible, varieties of subpersonhood ("savages" versus "barbarians," as earlier noted) corresponding to different variants of the Racial Contract (expropriation/slave/colonial). Thus Kipling's native could have more than one face—"half devil and half child"—so that while (for the expropriation contract) some kinds might simply have to be exterminated (as in the Americas, Australia, and South Africa), for others (as in the colonial contract) a paternalist guidance (as in colonial Africa and Asia) might lead them (as "minors") at least partway to civilization. But in all cases, the bottom line was that one was dealing with entities not on the same moral tier, incapable of autonomy and self-rule. "Negroes, Indians, and [Kaffirs] cannot bear democracy," concluded John Adams.[38] (Think of Tarzan and the Phantom, She and Sheena, white kings and queens ruling the black jungle, laying down the law to the lesser breeds without it.)

Moreover, the dynamic interrelation of the categorization

meant, as Hegelians would be quick to recognize, that the categories reciprocally determined each other. Being a person, being white, meant—definitionally—*not* being a subperson, not having the qualities that dragged one down to the next ontological level. In the ideal Kantian world of the raceless social contract, persons can exist in the abstract; in the non-ideal world of the naturalized Racial Contract, persons are necessarily related to subpersons. For these are identities as "contrapuntal ensembles," requiring their opposites, with the "secondariness" of subpersons being, as Said phrases it, "paradoxically, essential to the primariness of the European."[39]

Where slavery was practiced, as in the United States and the Americas, so that a sustained relation between races obtained, whiteness and blackness evolved in a forced intimacy of loathing in which they determined each other by negation and self-recognition in part *through the eyes of the other*. In his prizewinning book on the evolution of the idea of freedom, Orlando Patterson argues that freedom has been generated from the experience of slavery, that the slave establishes the norm for *humans*.[40] Part of the present-day problem in trying to assimilate black Americans into the body politic is the deep encoding in the national psyche of the notion that, as Toni Morrison points out, *Americanness* definitionally means whiteness; European immigrants who came to America in the late nineteenth–early twentieth centuries proved their assimilation by entering the club of whiteness, affirming their endorsement of the Racial Contract.[41] The longtime joke in the black community is that the first word the German or Scandinavian or Italian learns on Ellis Island fresh off the boat is "nigger." Black American, African American, is oxymoronic, while White American, Euro-American, is pleonastic. Whiteness is defined in part in respect to an oppositional darkness, so that white self-conceptions of identity, personhood, and self-respect are then intimately tied up with the repudiation of the black Other. No matter how poor one was, one was still able to affirm the whiteness that distinguished one from the subpersons on the other side of the color line.

There is also a cognitive dimension that is likewise continuous with the Aristotelian tradition. Historically the paradigm indicator of subpersonhood has been deficient rationality, the inability to exercise in full the characteristic classically thought of as distinguishing us from animals. For the social contract, a rough equality in men's cognitive powers or at least a necessary groundfloor capability of detecting the immanent moral structuring of the universe (natural law), or what is rationally required for social cooperation, is crucial to the argument. For the Racial Contract, correspondingly, a basic *in*equality is asserted in the capacity of different human groups to know the world and to detect natural law. Subpersons are deemed cognitively inferior, lacking in the essential rationality that would make them fully human.

In the early (theological) versions of the Racial Contract, this difference was spelled out in terms of heathen unwillingness to recognize God's word. One early seventeenth-century minister characterized Native Americans as "having little of Humanitie but shape, ignorant of Civilitie, of Arts, of Religion; more brutish than the beasts they hunt, more wild and unmanly [than] that unmanned wild Countrey, which they range rather than inhabite; captivated also to Satans tyranny."[42] In later, secular versions, it is a raced incapacity for rationality, abstract thought, cultural development, civilization in general (generating those dark cognitive spaces on Europe's mapping of the world). In philosophy one could trace this common thread through Locke's speculations on the incapacities of primitive minds, David Hume's denial that any other race but whites had created worthwhile civilizations, Kant's thoughts on the rationality differentials between blacks and whites, Voltaire's polygenetic conclusion that blacks were a distinct and less able species, John Stuart Mill's judgment that those races "in their nonage" were fit only for "despotism." The assumption of nonwhite intellectual inferiority was widespread, even if not always tricked out in the pseudoscientific apparatus that Darwinism would later make possible. Once this theoretical advance had been made, of course, there was a tremendous outpouring of attempts to put the norming on a quantifiable basis—a revitalized craniometry, claims about brain size and brain corrugations, measurings of facial angles, pronouncements about dolichocephalic and brachycephalic heads, recapitulationism, and finally, of course, IQ theory—the feature putatively correlated with intelligence varying, but the desired outcome of confirming nonwhite intellectual inferiority always achieved.[43]

The implications of this denial of equal intellectual and cognizing ability are various. Since, as mentioned, it precludes cultural achievement, it invites the intervention of those who are capable of culture. Since it precludes the moral development necessary for being a responsible moral and political agent, it precludes full membership in the polity. Since it precludes veridical perception of the world, it even precludes in some cases court testimony: slaves in the United States were not allowed to give evidence against their masters, nor could Australian Aborigines testify against the white settlers. In general, over a period of centuries, the governing epistemic principle could be stated as the requirement that—at least on controversial issues—nonwhite cognition has to be verified by white cognition to be accepted as valid. And it is permitted to override white cognition only in extreme and unusual circumstances (large numbers of consistent nonwhite witnesses, some kind of disorder in the cognizing capacities of the white epistemic agent, etc.). (Further complications involve a shift from straightforward biological racism to a more attenuated "cultural" racism, where partial membership in the epistemic community is granted based on the extent to which nonwhites show themselves capable of mastering white Western culture.)

Finally, the norming of the individual also involves a specific norming of the *body*, an aesthetic norming. Judgments of moral worth are obviously conceptually distinct from judgments of aesthetic worth, but there is a psychological tendency to conflate the two, as illustrated by the conventions of children's (and some adults') fairy tales, with their cast of handsome heroes, beautiful heroines, and ugly villains. Harmannus Hoetink argues that all societies have a "somatic norm image," deviation from which triggers alarms.[44] And George Mosse points out that the Enlightenment involved "the establishment of a stereotype of human beauty fashioned after classical models as the measure of all human worth. . . . Racism was a visual ideology based upon stereotypes. . . . Beauty and ugliness became as much principles of human classification as material factors of measurement, climate, and the environment."[45] The Racial Contract makes the white body the somatic norm, so that in early racist theories one finds not only moral but aesthetic judgments, with beautiful and fair races pitted against ugly and dark races. Some nonwhites were close enough to Caucasians in appearance that they were sometimes seen as beautiful, attractive in an exotic way (Native Americans on occasion; Tahitians; some Asians). But those more distant from the Caucasoid somatotype—paradigmatically blacks (Africans and also Australian Aborigines)—were stigmatized as aesthetically repulsive and deviant. Winthrop Jordan has documented the repelled fascination with which Englishmen discussed the appearance of the Africans they encountered in early trading expeditions, and Americans such as Thomas Jefferson expressed their antipathy to Negroid features.[46] (Benjamin Franklin, interestingly, opposed the slave trade on grounds that were at least partially aesthetic, as a kind of beautification program for America. Voicing his concern that importation of slaves had "blacken'd half America," he asked: "Why increase the Sons of Africa, by Planting them in America, where we have so fair an Opportunity, by excluding all Blacks and Tawneys, of increasing the lovely White and Red?")[47]

To the extent that these norms are accepted, blacks will be the race most alienated from their own bodies—a fate particularly painful for black women, who, like all women, will (by the terms, here, of the *Sexual* Contract) be valued chiefly by their physical appearance, which will generally be deemed to fall short of the Caucasoid or light-skinned ideal.[48] Moreover, apart from their obvious consequences for intra- and interracial sexual relationships, these norms will affect opportunities and employment prospects also, for studies have confirmed that a "pleasing" physical appearance gives one an edge in job competition. It is no accident that blacks of mixed race are those who are differentially represented in employment in the "white" world. They will, because of their background, often tend to be better educated also, but an additional factor is that whites are less physically uncomfortable with them. "If we have to hire any of them," it may be thought, "at least this one looks a bit like us."

The Racial Contract underwrites the modern social contract and is continually being rewritten.

Radical feminists argue that the oppression of women is the oldest oppression. Racial oppression is much more recent.

Whereas relations between the sexes necessarily go back to the origin of the species, an intimate and central relationship between Europe as a collective entity and non-Europe, "white" and "nonwhite" races, is a phenomenon of the *modern* epoch. There is ongoing scholarly controversy over the existence and extent of racism in antiquity ("racism" as a complex of ideas, that is, as against a developed politicoeconomic system), with some writers, such as Frank Snowden, finding a period "before color prejudice," in which blacks are obviously seen as equals, and others claiming that Greek and Roman bigotry against blacks was there from the beginning.[49] But obviously, whatever the disagreement on this point, it would have to be agreed that the ideology of modern racism is far more theoretically developed than ancient or medieval prejudices and is linked (whatever one's view, idealist or materialist, of causal priority) to a system of European domination.

Nevertheless, this divergence does imply that different accounts of the Racial Contract are possible. The account I favor conceives the Racial Contract as creating not merely racial exploitation, *but race itself* as a group identity. In a contemporary vocabulary, the Racial Contract "constructs" race. (For other accounts, for example, more essentialist ones, racial self-identification would *precede* the drawing up of the Racial Contract.) "White" people do not preexist but are brought into existence *as* "whites" by the Racial Contract—hence the peculiar transformation of the human population that accompanies this contract. The white race is *invented*, and one becomes "white by law."[50]

In this framework, then, the golden age of contract theory (1650 to 1800) overlapped with the growth of a European capitalism whose development was stimulated by the voyages of exploration that increasingly gave the contract a *racial* subtext. The evolution of the modern version of the contract, characterized by an antipatriarchalist Enlightenment liberalism, with its proclamations of the equal rights, autonomy, and freedom of all men, thus took place simultaneously with the massacre, expropriation, and subjection to hereditary slavery of men at least apparently human. This contradiction needs to be reconciled; it is reconciled through the Racial Contract, which essentially denies their personhood and restricts the terms of the social contract to whites. "To invade and dispossess the people of an unoffending civilized country would violate morality and transgress the principles of international law," writes Jennings, "but savages were exceptional. Being uncivilized by definition, they were outside the sanctions of both morality and law."[51] The *Racial* Contract is thus the truth of the *social* contract.

There is some direct evidence that it is in the writings of the classic contract theorists themselves. That is, it is not merely a matter of hypothetical intellectual reconstruction on my part, arguing from silence that "men" must really have meant "white men." Already Hugo Grotius, whose early seventeenth-century work on natural law provided the crucial theoretical background for later contractarians, gives, as Robert Williams has pointed out, the ominous judgment that for "barbarians," "wild beasts rather than men, one may rightly say . . . that the most just war is against savage beasts, the next against men who are like beasts."[52] But let us just focus on the four most important contract theorists: Hobbes, Locke, Rousseau, and Kant.[53]

Consider, to begin with, Hobbes's notoriously bestial state of nature, a state of war where life is "nasty, brutish, and short." On a superficial reading, it might seem that it is nonracial, equally applicable to everybody, but note what he says when considering the objection that "there was never such a time, nor condition of warre as this." He replies, "I believe it was never generally so, over all the world: but there are many places, where they live so now," his example being "the savage people in many places of *America*."[54] So a nonwhite people, indeed the very nonwhite people upon whose land his fellow Europeans were then encroaching, is his only real-life example of people in a state of nature. (And in fact, it has been pointed out that the phrasing and terminology of Hobbes's characterization may well have been derived directly from the writings of contemporaries about settlement in the Americas. The "explorer" Walter Raleigh described a civil war as "a state of War, which is the meer state of Nature of Men out of community, where all have an equal right to all things." And two other authors of the time characterized the inhabitants of the Americas as "people [who] lived like wild beasts, without religion, nor government, nor town, nor houses, without cultivating the land, nor clothing their bodies" and "people living yet as the first men, without letters, without lawes, without Kings, without common wealthes, without arts . . . not civil by nature.")[55]

In the next paragraph, Hobbes goes on to argue that "though there had never been any time, wherein particular men were in a condition of warre one against another," there is "in all times" a state of "continuall jealousies" between kings and persons of sovereign authority. He presumably emphasizes this contention in order for the reader to imagine what would happen in the absence of a "common Power to feare."[56] But the text is confusing. How could it simultaneously be the case that "there had never been" any such literal state-of-nature war, when in the previous paragraph he had just said that some *were* living like that now? As a result of this ambiguity, Hobbes has been characterized as a literal contractarian by some commentators and as a hypothetical contractarian by others. But I think this minor mystery can be cleared up once we recognize that there is a tacit racial logic in the text: the *literal* state of nature is reserved for nonwhites; for whites the state of nature is *hypothetical*. The conflict between whites is the conflict between those with *sovereigns*, that is, those who are already (and have always been) in society. From this conflict, one can extrapolate (gesturing at the racial abyss, so to speak) to what might happen in the absence of a ruling sovereign. But really we know that whites are too rational to allow this to happen to *them*. So the most notorious state of nature in the contractarian literature—the bestial war of all against all—is really a *nonwhite* figure, a racial object lesson for the more rational whites, whose superior grasp of natural law (here in its prudential rather than altruistic version) will enable them to take the necessary steps to avoid it and not to behave as "savages."

Hobbes has standardly been seen as an awkwardly transitional writer, caught between feudal absolutism and the rise of parliamentarianism, who uses the contract now classically associated with the emergence of liberalism to defend absolutism. But it might be argued that he is transitional in another way, in that in mid-seventeenth century Britain the imperial project was not yet so fully developed that the intellectual apparatus of racial subordination had been completely elaborated. Hobbes remains enough of a racial egalitarian that, while singling out Native Americans for his real-life example, he suggests that without a sovereign *even Europeans* could descend to their state, and that the absolutist government appropriate for nonwhites could also be appropriate for whites.[57] The uproar that greeted his work can be seen as attributable at least in part to this moral/political suggestion. The spread of colonialism would consolidate an intellectual world in which this bestial state of nature would be reserved for nonwhite savages, to be despotically governed, while civil Europeans would enjoy the benefits of liberal parliamentarianism. *The Racial Contract began to rewrite the social contract.*

One can see this transition more clearly by the time of Locke, whose state of nature is normatively regulated by traditional (altruistic, nonprudential) natural law. It is a moralized state of nature in which private property and money exist, indeed a state of nature that is virtually civil. Whites can thus be literally in this state of nature (for a brief period, anyway) without its calling into question their innate qualities. Locke famously argues that God gave the world "to the use of the Industrious and Rational," which qualities were indicated by labor. So while industrious and rational Englishmen were toiling away at home, in America, by contrast, one found "wild woods and uncultivated wast[e] . . . left to Nature" by the idle Indians.[58] Though they share the state of nature for a time with nonwhites, then, their residence is necessarily briefer, since whites, by appropriating and adding value to this natural world, exhibit their superior rationality. So the mode of appropriation of Native Americans is no real mode of appropriation at all, yielding property rights that can be readily overridden (if they exist at all), and thereby rendering their territories normatively open for seizure once those who have long since *left* the state of nature (Europeans) encounter them. Locke's thesis was in fact to be the central pillar of the expropriation contract—"the principal philosophical delineation of the normative arguments supporting white civilization's conquest of America," writes Williams[59]—and not merely in the United States but later in the other white settler states in Africa and the Pacific. Aboriginal economies did not improve the land and thus could be regarded as nonexistent.

The practice, and arguably also the theory, of Locke played a role in the slavery contract also. In the *Second Treatise*, Locke defends slavery resulting from a just war, for example, a defensive war against aggression. This would hardly be an accurate characterization of European raiding parties seeking African slaves, and in any case, in the same chapter Locke explicitly opposes hereditary slavery and the enslavement of wives and children.[60] Yet Locke had investments in the slave-trading Royal Africa Company and earlier assisted in writing the slave constitution of Carolina. So one could argue that the Racial Contract manifests itself here in an astonishing inconsistency, which could be resolved by the supposition that Locke saw blacks as not fully human and thus as subject to a different set of normative rules. Or perhaps the same Lockean moral logic that covered Native Americans can be extended to blacks also. They weren't appropriating their home continent of Africa; they're not rational; they can be enslaved.[61]

Rousseau's writings might seem to be something of an exception. After all, it is with his work that the notion of the "noble savage" is associated (though the phrase is not actually his own). And in the *Discourse on Inequality*'s reconstruction of the origins of society, everybody is envisaged as having been in the state of nature (and thus to have been "savage") at one time or another. But a careful reading of the text reveals, once again, crucial racial distinctions. The only natural savages cited are *nonwhite* savages, examples of European savages being restricted to reports of feral children raised by wolves and bears, child-rearing practices (we are told) comparable to those of Hottentots and Caribs.[62] (Europeans are so intrinsically civilized that it takes upbringing by animals to turn *them* into savages.) For Europe, savagery is in the dim distant past, since metallurgy and agriculture are the inventions leading to civilization, and it turns out that "one of the best reasons why Europe, if not the earliest to be civilized, has been at least more continuously and better civilized than other parts of the world, is perhaps that it is at once the richest in iron and the most fertile in wheat." But Rousseau was writing more than two hundred years after the European encounter with the great Aztec and Inca empires; wasn't there at least a little metallurgy and agriculture in evidence there? Apparently not: "Both metallurgy and agriculture were unknown to the savages of America, who have always therefore remained savages."[63] So even what might initially seem to be a more open environmental determinism, which would open the door to racial egalitarianism rather than racial hierarchy, degenerates into massive historical amnesia and factual misrepresentation, driven by the presuppositions of the Racial Contract.

Moreover, to make the obvious point, even if some of Rousseau's nonwhite savages are "noble," physically and psychologically healthier than the Europeans of the degraded and corrupt society produced by the real-life bogus contract, they are still *savages*. So they are primitive beings who are not actually part of civil society, barely raised above animals, without language. Leaving the state of nature, as Rousseau argues in *The Social Contract*, his later account of an ideal polity, is necessary for us to become fully human moral agents, beings capable of justice.[64] So the praise for nonwhite savages is a limited paternalistic praise, tantamount to admiration for healthy animals, in no way to be taken to imply their equality, let alone superiority, to the civilized Europeans of the ideal polity. The underlying racial dichotomization and hierarchy of civilized and savage remains quite clear.

Finally, Kant's version of the social contract is in a sense the best illustration of the grip of the Racial Contract on Europeans, since by this time the actual contract and the historical dimension of contractarianism had apparently vanished altogether. So here if anywhere, one would think—in this world of abstract persons, demarcated as such only by their rationality—race would have become irrelevant. But as

Emmanuel Eze has recently demonstrated in great detail, this orthodox picture is radically misleading, and the nature of Kantian "persons" and the Kantian "contract" must really be rethought.[65] For it turns out that Kant, widely regarded as the most important moral theorist of the modern period, in a sense the father of modern moral theory, and—through the work of John Rawls and Jürgen Habermas—increasingly central to modern political philosophy as well, is also the father of the modern concept of race.[66] His 1775 essay "The Different Races of Mankind" ("Von den Verschiedenen Rassen der Menschen") is a classic pro-hereditarian, antienvironmentalist statement of "the immutability and permanence of race." For him, comments George Mosse, "racial make-up becomes an unchanging substance and the foundation of all physical appearance and human development, including intelligence."[67] The famous theorist of personhood is also the theorist of subpersonhood, though this distinction is, in what the suspicious might almost think a conspiracy to conceal embarrassing truths, far less well known.

As Eze points out, Kant taught anthropology and physical geography for forty years, and his philosophical work really has to be read *in conjunction with these lectures* to understand how racialized his views on moral character were. His notorious comment in *Observations on the Feeling of the Beautiful and Sublime* is well known to, and often cited by, black intellectuals: "So fundamental is the difference between [the black and white] races of man . . . it appears to be as great in regard to mental capacities as in color" so that "a clear proof that what [a Negro] said was stupid" was that "this fellow was quite black from head to foot."[68] The point of Eze's essay is that this remark is by no means isolated or a casual throwaway line that, though of course regrettable, has no broader implications. Rather, it comes out of a developed theory of race and corresponding intellectual ability and limitation. It only *seems* casual, unembedded in a larger theory, because white academic philosophy as an institution has had no interest in researching, pursuing the implications of, and making known to the world this dimension of Kant's work.

In fact, Kant demarcates and theorizes a color-coded racial hierarchy of Europeans, Asians, Africans, and Native Americans, differentiated by their degree of innate *talent*. Eze explains: "'Talent' is that which, by 'nature,' guarantees for the 'white,' in Kant's racial rational and moral order, the highest position above all creatures, followed by the 'yellow,' the 'black,' and then the 'red.' Skin color for Kant is evidence of superior, inferior, or no 'gift' of 'talent,' or the capacity to realize reason and rational-moral perfectibility through education. . . . It cannot, therefore, be argued that skin color for Kant was merely a physical characteristic. It is, rather, evidence of an unchanging and unchangeable moral quality." Europeans, to no one's surprise I presume, have all the necessary talents to be morally self-educating; there is some hope for Asians, though they lack the ability to develop abstract concepts; the innately idle Africans can at least be educated as servants and slaves through the instruction of a split-bamboo cane (Kant gives some useful advice on how to beat Negroes efficiently); and the wretched Native Americans are just hopeless, and cannot be educated at all. So, in complete opposition to the image of his work that has come down to us and is standardly taught in introductory ethics courses, full personhood for Kant is actually dependent upon race. In Eze's summary, "The black person, for example, can accordingly be denied full humanity since full and 'true' humanity accrues only to the white European."[69]

The recent furor about Paul de Man[70] and, decades earlier, Martin Heidegger, for their complicity with the Nazis, thus needs to be put into perspective. These are essentially bit players, minor leaguers. One needs to distinguish theory from actual practice, of course, and I'm not saying that Kant would have endorsed genocide. *But the embarrassing fact for the white West (which doubtless explains its concealment) is that their most important moral theorist of the past three hundred years is also the foundational theorist in the modern period of the division between* Herrenvolk *and* Untermenschen, *persons and subpersons, upon which Nazi theory would later draw.* Modern moral theory and modern racial theory have the same father.

The Racial Contract, therefore, underwrites the social contract, is a visible or hidden operator that restricts and modifies the scope of its prescriptions. But since there is both synchronic and diachronic variation, there are many different versions or local instantiations of the Racial Contract, and they evolve over time, so that the effective force of the social contract itself changes, and the kind of cognitive dissonance between the two alters. (This change has implications for the moral psychology of the white signatories and their characteristic patterns of insight and blindness.) The social contract is (in its original historical version) a specific discrete event that founds society, even if (through, e.g., Lockean theories of tacit consent) subsequent generations continue to ratify it on an ongoing basis. By contrast the Racial Contract is *continually being rewritten* to create different forms of the racial polity.

A global periodization, a timeline overview of the evolution of the Racial Contract, would highlight first of all the crucial division between the time before and the time after the institutionalization of global white supremacy. (Thus Janet Abu-Lughod's book about the thirteenth-century/fourteenth-century medieval world system is titled *Before European Hegemony*.)[71] The time after would then be further subdivided into the period of formal, juridical white supremacy (the epoch of the European conquest, African slavery, and European colonialism, overt white racial self-identification, and the largely undisputed hegemony of racist theories) and the present period of de facto white supremacy, when whites' dominance is, for the most part, no longer constitutionally and juridically enshrined but rather a matter of social, political, cultural, and economic privilege based on the legacy of the conquest.

In the first period, the period of de jure white supremacy, the Racial Contract was explicit, the characteristic instantiations—the expropriation contract, the slave contract, the colonial contract—making it clear that whites were the privileged race and the egalitarian social contract applied only to them. (Cognitively, then, this period had the great virtue of social transparency: white supremacy was *openly* proclaimed. One didn't have to look for a *sub*text, because it was there in the text itself.) In the second period, on the other hand, the Racial Contract *has written itself out of formal existence.* The scope of the terms in the social contract has been formally extended to apply to everyone, so that "persons" is no longer coextensive with "whites." What characterizes *this* period (which is, of course, the present) is tension between continuing de facto white privilege and this *formal* extension of rights. The Racial Contract continues to manifest itself, of course, in unofficial local agreements of various kinds (restrictive covenants, employment discrimination contracts, political decisions about resource allocation, etc.). But even apart from these, a crucial manifestation is simply *the failure to ask certain questions,* taking for granted as a status quo and baseline the existing color-coded configurations of wealth, poverty, property, and opportunities, the pretence that formal, juridical equality is sufficient to remedy inequities created on a foundation of several hundred years of racial privilege, and that challenging that foundation is a transgression of the terms of the social contract. (Though actually—in a sense—it *is*, insofar as the Racial Contract is the real meaning of the social contract.)

Globally, the Racial Contract effects a final paradoxical norming and racing of space, a *writing out* of the polity of certain spaces as conceptually and historically irrelevant to European and Euro-world development, so that these raced spaces are categorized as disjoined from the path of civilization (i.e., the European project). Fredric Jameson writes: "Colonialism means that a significant structural segment of the economic system as a whole is now located elsewhere, beyond the metropolis, outside of the daily life and existential experience of the home country. . . . Such spatial disjunction has as its immediate consequence the inability to grasp the way the system functions as a whole."[72] By the social contract's decision to remain in the space of the European nation-state, the connection between the development of this space's industry, culture, civilization, and the material and cultural contributions of Afro-Asia and the Americas is denied, so it seems as if this space and its denizens are peculiarly rational and industrious, differentially endowed with qualities that have enabled them to dominate the world. One then speaks of the "European miracle" in a way that conceives this once marginal region as sui generis, conceptually severing it from the web of spatial connections that made its development possible. *This* space actually comes to have the character it does because of the pumping exploitative causality established between it and those *other* conceptually invisible spaces. But by remaining within the boundaries of the European space of the abstract contract, it is valorized as unique, inimitable, autonomous. Other parts of the world then disappear from the white contractarian history, subsumed under the general category of risible non-European space, the "Third World," where for reasons of local folly and geographical blight the inspiring model of the self-sufficient white social contract cannot be followed.

Nationally, within these racial polities, the Racial Contract manifests itself in white resistance to anything more than the *formal* extension of the terms of the abstract social contract (and often to that also). Whereas before it was denied that nonwhites *were* equal persons, it is now pretended that nonwhites *are* equal abstract persons who can be fully included in the polity merely by extending the scope of the moral operator, without any fundamental change in the arrangements that have resulted from the previous system of explicit de jure racial privilege. Sometimes the new forms taken by the Racial Contract are transparently exploitative, for example, the "jim crow" contract, whose claim of "separate but equal" was patently ludicrous. But others—the job discrimination contract, the restrictive covenant—are harder to prove. Employment agencies use subterfuges of various kinds: "In 1990, for example, two former employees of one of New York City's largest employment agencies divulged that discrimination was routinely practiced against black applicants, though concealed behind a number of code words. Clients who did not want to hire blacks would indicate their preference for applicants who were 'All American.' For its part the agency would signal that an applicant was black by reversing the initials of the placement counselor."[73] Similarly, a study of how "American apartheid" is maintained points out that whereas in the past realtors would have simply refused to sell to blacks, now blacks "are met by a realtor with a smiling face who, through a series of ruses, lies, and deceptions, makes it hard for them to learn about, inspect, rent, or purchase homes in white neighborhoods. . . . Because the discrimination is latent, however, it is usually unobservable, even to the person experiencing it. One never knows for sure."[74] Nonwhites then find that race is, paradoxically, both everywhere and nowhere, structuring their lives but not formally recognized in political/moral theory. But in a racially structured polity, the only people who can find it psychologically possible to deny the centrality of race are those who are racially privileged, for whom race is invisible precisely because the world is structured around them, whiteness as the ground against which the figures of other races—those who, unlike us, are raced—appear. The fish does not see the water, and whites do not see the racial nature of a white polity because it is natural to them, the element in which they move. As Toni Morrison points out, there are contexts in which claiming racelessness is itself a racial act.[75]

Contemporary debates between nonwhites and whites about the centrality or peripherality of race can thus be seen as attempts respectively to point out, and deny, the existence of the Racial Contract that underpins the social contract. The frustrating problem nonwhites have always had, and continue to have, with mainstream political theory is not with abstraction *itself* (after all, the "Racial Contract" is itself an abstraction) but with an *idealizing* abstraction that abstracts *away* from the crucial realities of the racial polity.[76] The shift to the hypothetical, ideal contract encourages and facilitates this abstraction, since the eminently *non*ideal features of the real world are not part of the apparatus. There is then, in a sense, no conceptual point-of-entry to start talking about the fundamental way in which (as all nonwhites know) race structures one's life and affects one's life chances.

The black law professor Patricia Williams complains about an ostensible neutrality that is really "racism in drag," a system of "racism as status quo" which is "deep, angry, eradicated from view" but continues to make people "avoid the phantom as they did the substance," "defer[ring] to the unseen shape of things."[77] The black philosophy professor Bill Lawson comments on the deficiencies of the conceptual apparatus of traditional liberalism, which has no room for the peculiar post-Emancipation status of blacks, simultaneously citizens and noncitizens.[78] The black philosopher of law Anita Allen remarks on the irony of standard American philosophy of law texts, which describe a universe in which "all humans are paradigm rightsholders" and see no need to point out that the actual U.S. record is somewhat different.[79] The retreat of mainstream normative moral and political theory into an "ideal" theory that ignores race merely rescripts the Racial Contract as the invisible writing between the lines. So John Rawls, an American working in the late twentieth century, writes a book on justice widely credited with reviving postwar political philosophy in which not a single reference to American slavery and its legacy can be found, and Robert Nozick creates a theory of justice in holdings predicated on legitimate acquisition and transfer without more than two or three sentences acknowledging the utter divergence of U.S. history from this ideal.[80]

The silence of mainstream moral and political philosophy on issues of race is a sign of the continuing power of the Contract over its signatories, an illusory color blindness that actually entrenches white privilege. A genuine transcendence of its terms would require, as a preliminary, the acknowledgment of its past and present existence and the social, political, economic, psychological, and moral implications it has had both for its contractors and its victims. By treating the present as a somehow neutral baseline, with its given configuration of wealth, property, social standing, and psychological willingness to sacrifice, the idealized social contract renders permanent the legacy of the Racial Contract. The ever-deepening abyss between the First World and the Third World, where millions—largely nonwhite—die of starvation each year and many more hundreds of millions—also largely nonwhite— live in wretched poverty, is seen as unfortunate (calling, certainly, for the occasional charitable contribution) but unrelated to the history of transcontinental and intracontinental racial exploitation.

Finally, the Racial Contract evolves not merely by altering the relations between whites and nonwhites but by shifting the criteria for who *counts* as white and nonwhite. (So it is not merely that relations between the respective populations change but that the population boundaries themselves change also.) Thus—at least in my preferred account of the Racial Contract (again, other accounts are possible)—race is *debiologized*, making explicit its political foundation. *In a sense, the Racial Contract constructs its signatories as much as they construct it.* The overall trend is toward a limited expansion of the privileged human population through the "whitening" of the previously excluded group in question, though there may be local reversals.

The Nazi project can then be seen in part as the attempt to turn the clock back by rewriting a more exclusivist version of the Racial Contract than was globally acceptable at the time. (One writer suggests ironically that this was "the attempt of the Germans to make themselves masters of the master race.")[81] And this backtracking leads to a problem. My categorization (white/nonwhite, person/subperson) has the virtues of elegance and simplicity and seems to me to map the essential features of the racial polity accurately, to carve the social reality at its ontological joints. But since, as a pair of contradictories, this categorization is jointly exhaustive of the possibilities, it raises the question of where to locate what could be called "borderline" Europeans, white people with a question mark—the Irish, Slavs, Mediterraneans, and above all, of course, Jews. In the colonial wars with Ireland, the English routinely used derogatory imagery—"savages," "cannibals," "bestial appearance"—that it would now seem incredible to apply to whites.[82] The wave of mid-nineteenth-century Irish immigration into the United States stimulated one wit to observe that "it would be a good thing if every Irishman were to kill a nigger and then be hung for it," and caricatures in the newspapers often represented the Irish as simian. European racism against nonwhites has been my focus, but there were also *intra*-European varieties of "racism"—Teutonism, Anglo-Saxonism, Nordicism—which are today of largely antiquarian interest but which were sufficiently influential in the 1920s that U.S. immigration law favored "Nordics" over "Mediterraneans." (There is some recognition of this distinction in popular culture. *Cheers* fans will remember that the "Italian" waitress Carla [Rhea Perlman], curly haired and swarthy, sometimes calls the blond, "alabaster-skinned" WASP Diane [Shelley Long] "Whitey," and in the 1992 movie *Zebrahead,* two black teenagers discuss the question of whether Italians are *really* white.) Finally, Jews, of course, have been the victims of Christian Europe's anti-Semitic discrimination and pogroms since medieval times, this record of persecution reaching its horrific climax under the Third Reich.

How, then, should these Europeans be categorized, given the white/nonwhite dichotomization? One solution would be to reject it for a three- or four-way division. But I am reluctant to do so, since I think the dyadic partition really does capture the essential structure of the global racial polity. My solution therefore is to retain but "fuzzify" the categories, introducing internal distinctions within them. I have already pointed out that some nonwhites ("barbarians" as against "savages") ranked higher than others; for example, the Chinese and (Asian) Indians would have been placed above Africans and Australian

Aborigines. So it would seem that one could also rank whites, and in fact Winthrop Jordan notes that "if Europeans were white, some were whiter than others."[83] All whites are equal, then, but some are whiter, and so more equal, than others, and all nonwhites are unequal, but some are blacker, and so more unequal, than others. The fundamental conceptual cut, the primary division, then remains that between whites and nonwhites, and the fuzzy status of inferior whites is accommodated by the category of "off-white" rather than nonwhite. Commenting on the failure of the "valiant efforts of the English to turn their ethnocentric feelings of superiority over the 'black' Irish into racism," Richard Drinnon concludes that "the Celts remained at most *white* niggers' in their eyes."[84] And with the exception of Nazi Germany, to be discussed later, this seems to me a judgment that could be generalized for all these cases of borderline Europeans—that they were not subpersons in the full technical sense and would all have been ranked ontologically above genuine nonwhites. The ease with which they have now been assimilated into postwar Europe and accepted as full whites in the United States is some evidence for the correctness of this way of drawing the distinction.

Nevertheless, these problem cases are useful in illustrating—against essentialists—the social rather than biological basis of the Racial Contract. Phenotypical whiteness and European origin were not always sufficient for *full* Whiteness, acceptance into the inner sanctum of the racial club, and the rules had to be rewritten to permit inclusion. (One recent book, for example, bears the title *How the Irish Became White*.)[85] On the other hand, there are groups "clearly" not white who have conjuncturally come to be seen as such. The Japanese were classified as "honorary whites" for the purpose of the Axis alliance, the restrictive, local Racial Contract (as they were in South Africa under apartheid), while being classified as verminous nonwhites with respect to the Western Allies, inheritors of the global Racial Contract.[86] A century ago, at the time of the European domination of China and the Boxer rebellion, the Chinese were a degraded race, signs were posted saying "No dogs or Chinese allowed," and they faced heavy immigration restrictions and discrimination in the United States. "Yellow Peril" depictions of Chinese in the American popular media in the early twentieth century included the sinister Orientals of Sax Rohmer's Fu Manchu novels and the Ming the Merciless nemesis of Flash Gordon. But today in the United States, Asians are seen as a "model minority," even (according to Andrew Hacker) "probationary whites," who might make it if they hang in there long enough. "Is Yellow Black or White?" asks one Asian American historian; the answer varies.[87] The point, then, is that the membership requirements for Whiteness are rewritten over time, with shifting criteria prescribed by the evolving Racial Contract.

The Racial Contract has to be enforced through violence and ideological conditioning.

The social contract is, by definition, classically voluntaristic, modeling the polity on a basis of individualized consent. What justifies the authority of the state over us is that "we the people" *agreed* to give it that authority. (On the older, "feudal" patriarchal model, by contrast—the model of Sir Robert Filmer, Locke's target in the *Second Treatise*—people were represented as being *born into* subordination.)[88] The legitimacy of the state derives from the freely given consent of the signatories to transfer or delegate their rights to it, and its role in the mainstream moralized/constitutionalist version of the contract (Lockean/Kantian) is, correspondingly, to protect those rights and safeguard the welfare of its citizens. The liberal-democratic state is then an ethical state, whether in the minimalist, night-watchman Lockean version of enforcing noninterference with citizens' rights or in the more expansive redistributivist version of actively promoting citizens' welfare. In both cases the liberal state is neutral in the sense of not privileging some citizens over others. Correspondingly, the laws that are passed have as their rationale this juridical regulation of the polity for generally acceptable moral ends.

This idealized model of the liberal-democratic state has, of course, been challenged from various political directions over the past century or so: the recently revived Hegelian moral critique from the perspective of a competing, allegedly superior ideal, a *communitarian* state seeking actively to promote a common conception of the good; the degraded version of this in the fascist *corporatist* state; the anarchist challenge to *all* states as usurping bodies of legitimized violence; and what has been the most influential radical critique up till recently, the Marxist analysis of the state as an instrument of class power, so that the liberal-democratic state is supposedly unmasked as the *bourgeois* state, the state of the ruling class.

My claim is that the model of the Racial Contract shows us that we need another alternative, another way of theorizing about and critiquing the state: the *racial*, or white-supremacist, state, whose function inter alia is to safeguard the polity *as* a white or white-dominated polity, enforcing the terms of the Racial Contract by the appropriate means and, when necessary, facilitating its rewriting from one form to another.

The liberal-democratic state of classic contractarianism abides by the terms of the social contract by using force only to protect its citizens, who delegated this moralized force to it so that it could guarantee the safety not to be found in the state of nature. (This was, after all, part of the whole point of *leaving* the state of nature in the first place.) By contrast, the state established by the Racial Contract is by definition *not* neutral, since its purpose is to bring about conformity to the terms of the Racial Contract among the subperson population, which will obviously have no reason to accept these terms voluntarily, since the contract is an exploitation contract. (An alternative, perhaps even superior, formulation might be: it *is* neutral for its full citizens, who are white, but as a corollary, it is nonneutral toward the nonwhites, whose intrinsic savagery constantly threatens reversion to the state of nature, bubbles of wilderness within the polity, as I suggested.)

Of necessity, then, this state treats whites and nonwhites, persons and subpersons, differently, though in later variants of the Racial Contract it is necessary to conceal this difference. In seeking first to establish and later to reproduce itself, the racial state employs the two traditional weapons of coercion: physical violence and ideological conditioning.

In the early phase of establishing global white supremacy, overt physical violence was, of course, the dominant face of this political project: the genocide of Native Americans in the conquest of the two continents and of Aborigines in Australia; the punitive colonial wars in Africa, Asia, and the Pacific; the incredible body counts of slaving expeditions, the Middle Passage, "seasoning," and slavery itself; the state-supported seizure of lands and imposition of regimes of forced labor. In the expropriation contract, the subpersons are either killed or placed on reservations, so that extensive daily intercourse with them is not necessary; they are not part of the white polity proper. In the slavery and colonial contracts, on the other hand, persons and subpersons necessarily interact regularly, so that constant watchfulness for signs of subperson

83

resistance to the terms of the Racial Contract is required. If
the social contract is predicated on voluntarized compliance,
the Racial Contract clearly requires compulsion for the repro-
duction of the political system. In the slavery contract, in
particular, the terms of the contract require of the slave an
ongoing self-negation of personhood, an acceptance of chattel
status, psychologically harder to achieve and so potentially
more explosive than the varieties of subpersonhood imposed
either by the expropriation contract (where one will either be
dead or sequestered in a space far away from white persons)
or the colonial contract (where the status of "minor" leaves
some hope that one may be permitted to achieve adulthood
some day). Thus, in the Caribbean and on the mainland of the
Americas, there were sites where newly arrived Africans were
sometimes taken to be "seasoned" before being transported
to the plantations. And this was basically the metaphysical
operation, carried out through the physical, of *breaking* them,
transforming them from persons into subpersons of the chattel
variety. But since people could always fake acceptance of subpersonhood, it was, of course, necessary to keep an eternally
vigilant eye on them for possible signs of dissembling, in keeping with the sentiment that eternal vigilance is the price of
freedom.

The coercive arms of the state, then—the police, the penal
system, the army—need to be seen as in part the enforcers *of*
the Racial Contract, working both to keep the peace and prevent crime among the white citizens, and to maintain the
racial order and detect and destroy challenges to it, so that
across the white settler states nonwhites are incarcerated at
differential rates and for longer terms. To understand the long,
bloody history of police brutality against blacks in the United
States, for example, one has to recognize it not as excesses
by individual racists but as an organic part of this political

enterprise. There is a well-known perception in the black community that the police—particularly in the jim crow days of segregation and largely white police forces—were basically an "army of occupation."

Correspondingly, in all these white and white-ruled polities, attacking or killing whites has always been morally and juridically singled out as the crime of crimes, a horrific break with the natural order, not merely because of the greater value of white (i.e., a person's) life but because of its larger symbolic significance as a challenge to the racial polity. The death penalty is differentially applied to nonwhites both in the scope of crimes covered (i.e., racially differentiated penalties for the same crimes)[89] and in its actual carrying out. (In the history of U.S. capital punishment, for example, over one thousand people have been executed, but only very rarely has a white been executed for killing a black.)[90] Individual acts of subperson violence against whites and, even more serious, slave rebellions and colonial uprisings are standardly punished in an exemplary way, *pour encourager les autres*, with torture and retaliatory mass killings far exceeding the number of white victims. Such acts have to be seen not as arbitrary, not as the product of individual sadism (though they encourage and provide an outlet for it), but as the appropriate moral and political response—prescribed by the Racial Contract—to a threat to a system predicated on nonwhite subpersonhood. There is an outrage that is practically metaphysical because one's self-conception, one's white identity as a superior being entitled to rule, is under attack.

Thus in the North and South American reactions to Native American resistance and slave uprisings, in the European responses to the Saint Domingue (Haitian) revolution, the Sepoy uprising ("Indian Mutiny"), the Jamaican Morant Bay insurrection, the Boxer rebellion in China, the struggle of the Hereros

85

in German Africa, in the twentieth century colonial and neo-colonial wars (Ethiopia, Madagascar, Vietnam, Algeria, Malaya, Kenya, Angola, Mozambique, Guinea-Bissau, Namibia), in the white settlers' battles to maintain a white Rhodesia and an apartheid South Africa, one repeatedly sees the same pattern of systematic massacre. It is a pattern that confirms that an *ontological shudder* has been sent through the system of the white polity, calling forth what could be called *the white terror* to make sure that the foundations of the moral and political universe stay in place. Describing the "shock to white America" of the Sioux defeat of Custer's Seventh Cavalry, one author writes: "It was the kind of humiliating defeat that simply could not be handed to a modern nation of 40 million people by a few scarecrow savages."[91] V. G. Kiernan comments on Haiti: "No savagery that has been recorded of Africans anywhere could outdo some of the acts of the French in their efforts to regain control of the island." Of the Indian Mutiny, he writes, "After victory there were savage reprisals. For the first time on such a scale, but not the last, the West was trying to quell the East by frightfulness. . . . Some of the facts that have come down to us almost stagger belief, even after the horrors of Europe's own twentieth-century history."[92] In general, then, watchfulness for nonwhite resistance and a corresponding readiness to employ massively disproportionate retaliatory violence are intrinsic to the fabric of the racial polity in a way different from the response to the typical crimes of white citizens.

But official state violence is not the only sanction of the Racial Contract. In the Lockean state of nature, in the absence of a constituted juridical and penal authority, natural law permits individuals themselves to punish wrongdoers. Those who show by their actions that they lack or have "renounced" the reason of natural law and are like "wild Savage Beasts, with whom Men can have no Society nor Security," may licitly be destroyed.[93] But if in the racial polity nonwhites may be regarded as *inherently* bestial and savage (quite independently of what they happen to be doing at any particular moment), then by extension they can be conceptualized in part as *carrying the state of nature around with them*, incarnating wildness and wilderness in their person. In effect, they can be regarded even in civil society as being potentially at the center of a mobile free-fire zone in which citizen-to-citizen/white-on-white moral and juridical constraints do not obtain. Particularly in frontier situations, where official White authority is distant or unreliable, individual whites may be regarded as endowed with the authority to enforce the Racial Contract themselves. Thus in the United States paradigmatically (but also in the European settlement in Australia, in the colonial outpost in the "bush" or "jungle" of Asia and Africa) there is a long history of vigilantism and lynching at which white officialdom basically connived, inasmuch as hardly anybody was ever punished, though the perpetrators were well known and on occasion photographs were even available. (Some lynchings were advertised days in advance, and hundreds or thousands of people gathered from surrounding districts.)[94] In the Northern Territory of Australia, one government medical officer wrote in 1901, "It was notorious that the blackfellows were shot down like crows and that no notice was taken."[95]

The other dimension of this coercion is ideological. If the Racial Contract creates its signatories, those party to the Contract, by constructing them as "white persons," it also tries to make its victims, the objects of the Contract, *into* the "nonwhite subpersons" it specifies. This project requires labor at *both* ends, involving the development of a depersonizing conceptual apparatus through which whites must learn to see nonwhites and also, crucially, through which nonwhites must learn to see themselves. For the nonwhites, then, this is something like the intellectual equivalent of the physical process of "seasoning," "slave breaking," the aim being to produce an entity who accepts subpersonhood. Frederick Douglass, in his famous first autobiography, describes the need to "darken [the] moral and mental vision, and, as far as possible, to annihilate the power of reason" of the slave: "He must be able to detect no inconsistencies in slavery; he must be made to feel that slavery is right; and he can be brought to that only when he ceases to be a man."[96] Originally denied education, blacks were later, in the postbellum period, given an education appropriate to postchattel status—the denial of a past, of history, of achievement—so that as far as possible they would accept their prescribed roles of servant and menial laborer, comic coons and Sambos, grateful Uncle Toms and Aunt Jemimas. Thus in one of the most famous books from the black American experience, Carter Woodson indicts "the mis-education of the Negro."[97] And as late as the 1950s, James Baldwin could declare that the "separate but equal" system of segregation "has worked brilliantly," for "it has allowed white people, with scarcely any pangs of conscience whatever, to *create*, in every generation, only the Negro they wished to see."[98]

In the case of Native Americans, whose resistance was largely over by the 1870s, a policy of cultural assimilation was introduced under the slogan "Kill the Indian, but save the man," aimed at the suppression and eradication of native religious beliefs and ceremonies, such as the Sioux Sun Dance.[99] Similarly, a hundred years later, Daniel Cabixi, a Brazilian Pareci Indian, complains that "the missions kill us from within. . . . They impose upon us another religion, belittling the values we hold. This decharacterises us to the point where we are ashamed to be Indians."[100] The Mohawk scholar Jerry Gambill lists "Twenty-one ways to 'scalp' an Indian," the first being "Make him a non-person. Human rights are for people. Convince Indians their ancestors were savages, that they were pagan."[101] Likewise, in the colonial enterprise, children in the Caribbean, Africa, and Asia were taught out of British or French or Dutch schoolbooks to see themselves as aspirant (but, of course, never full) colored Europeans, saved from the barbarities of their own cultures by colonial intervention, duly reciting "our ancestors, the Gauls," and growing up into adults with "black skin, white masks."[102] Australian Aborigine students write: **"Black is,** wronged at white schools but righted by experience. . . . **Black is,** going to white school and coming home again no wiser."[103] Ngũgĩ wa Thiong'o describes, from his experience in his native Kenya, the "cultural bomb" of British imperialism, which prohibited learning in the oral tradition of Gikuyu and trained him and his schoolfellows to see themselves and their country through the alien eyes of H. Rider Haggard and John Buchan: "The effect of a cultural bomb is to annihilate a people's belief in their names, in their languages, in their environment, in their heritage of struggle, in their unity, in their capacities and ultimately in themselves. It makes them see their past as one wasteland of non-achievement and it makes them want to distance themselves from that wasteland."[104] Racism as an ideology needs to be understood as aiming at the minds of nonwhites as well as whites, inculcating subjugation. If the social contract requires that all citizens and persons learn to respect themselves and each other, the Racial Contract prescribes nonwhite self-loathing and racial deference to white citizens. The ultimate triumph of this education is that it eventually becomes possible to characterize the Racial Contract as "consensual" and "voluntaristic" even for nonwhites.

"NATURALIZED" MERITS

inally, I want to point out the merits of this model as a "naturalized" account of the actual historical record, one which has explanatory as well as normative aspirations. Arguably, we are in a better position to *bring about* the (supposedly) desired political ideals if we can identify and explain the obstacles to their realization. In tracking the actual moral consciousness of most white agents, in depicting the actual political realities nonwhites have always recognized, the theory of the "Racial Contract" shows its superiority to the ostensibly abstract and general, but actually "white," social contract.

The Racial Contract historically tracks the actual moral/political consciousness of (most) white moral agents.

Moral theory, being a branch of value theory, traditionally deals with the realm of the ideal, norms to which we must try to live up as moral agents. And political philosophy is nowadays conceived of as basically an application of ethics to the social and political realm. So it is supposed to be dealing with ideals also. But in the first two chapters of this book, I have spent a great deal of time talking about the *actual* historical record and the *actual* norms and ideals that have prevailed in recent global history. I have been giving what, in the current jargon of philosophers, would be called a "naturalized" account, rather than an idealized account. And that is why I said from the beginning that I preferred the classic use of contract, which is seeking to describe and explain as well as to prescribe. But if ethics and political philosophy are focused on norms we want to endorse (ideal ideals, so to speak), what really was the point of this exercise? What would be the point of "naturalizing" ethics, which is explicitly the realm of the ideal?

My suggestion is that by looking at the *actual* historically dominant moral/political consciousness and the *actual* historically dominant moral/political ideals, we are better enabled to prescribe for society than by starting from ahistorical abstractions. In other words, the point is not to endorse this deficient consciousness and these repugnant ideals but, by recognizing their past and current influence and power and identifying their sources, to correct for them. Realizing a better future requires not merely admitting the ugly truth of the past—and present—but understanding the ways in which these realities were made invisible, acceptable to the white population. We want to know—both to describe and to explain—the circumstances that actually blocked achievement of the ideal raceless ideals and promoted instead the naturalized nonideal racial ideals. We want to know what went wrong in the past, is going wrong now, and is likely to *continue* to go wrong in the future if we do not guard against it.

Now by its relative silence on the question of race, conventional moral theory would lead the unwary student with no experience of the world—the visiting anthropologist from Galactic Central, say—to think that deviations from the ideal have been contingent, random, theoretically opaque, or not worth the trouble to theorize. Such a visitor might conclude that all people have generally tried to live up to the norm but, given inevitable human frailty, have sometimes fallen short. But this conclusion is, in fact, simply false. Racism and racially structured discrimination have not been *deviations* from the norm; they have *been* the norm, not merely in the sense of de facto statistical distribution patterns but, as I emphasized at the start, in the sense of being formally codified, written down and proclaimed *as such*. From this perspective, the Racial Contract has underwritten the social contract, so that duties, rights, and liberties have routinely been assigned on a racially differentiated basis. To understand the actual moral practice of past and present, one needs not merely the standard abstract discussions of, say, the conflicts in people's consciences between self-interest and empathy with others but a frank appreciation of how the Racial Contract creates a *racialized* moral psychology. Whites will then act in racist ways *while* thinking of themselves as acting morally. In other words, they will experience genuine cognitive difficulties in recognizing certain behavior patterns *as* racist, so that quite apart from questions of motivation and bad faith they will be morally handicapped simply from the conceptual point of view in seeing and doing the right thing. As I emphasized at the start, the Racial Contract prescribes, as a condition for membership in the polity, an epistemology of ignorance.

Feminist political philosophers have documented the striking uniformity of opinion among the classic male theorists on the subordination of women, so that as polar as their positions may be on other political or theoretical questions, there is common agreement on this. Plato the idealist and Aristotle the materialist agree that women should be subordinate, as

do Hobbes the absolutist and Rousseau the radical democrat.[1]
With the Racial Contract, as we have seen, there is a similar
pattern, among the contractarians Hobbes, Locke, Rousseau,
Kant, and their theoretical adversaries—the anticontractarian
Hume, who denies that any race other than the white one has
produced a civilization; the utilitarian Mill, who denies the
applicability of his antipaternalist "harm principle" to "barbarians" and maintains that they need European colonial despotism; the historicist G. W. F. Hegel, who denies that Africa
has any history and suggests that blacks were morally im-
proved through being enslaved.[2] So the Racial Contract is "or-
thogonal" to the varying directions of their thought, the
common assumption they can all take for granted, no matter
what their theoretical divergences on other questions. There
is also the evidence of silence. Where is Grotius's magisterial
*On Natural Law and the Wrongness of the Conquest of the
Indies*, Locke's stirring *Letter concerning the Treatment of
the Indians*, Kant's moving *On the Personhood of Negroes*,
Mill's famous condemnatory *Implications of Utilitarianism
for English Colonialism*, Karl Marx and Frederick Engels's
outraged *Political Economy of Slavery*?[3] Intellectuals write
about what interests them, what they find important, and—
especially if the writer is prolific—silence constitutes good
prima facie evidence that the subject was not of particular
interest. By their failure to denounce the great crimes insepa-
rable from the European conquest, or by the halfheartedness
of their condemnation, or by their actual endorsement of it
in some cases, most of the leading European ethical theorists
reveal their complicity in the Racial Contract.

What we need to do, then, is to identify and learn to understand the workings of a racialized ethic. How were people able
consistently to do the wrong thing while thinking that they
were doing the right thing? In part, it is a problem of cognition

and of white moral cognitive dysfunction. As such, it can potentially be studied by the new research program of cognitive science. For example, a useful recent survey article on "naturalizing" ethics by Alvin Goldman suggests three areas in which cognitive science may have implications for moral theory: (a) the "cognitive materials" used in moral thinking, such as the logic of concept application, and their possible determination by the cultural environment of the agent; (b) judgments about subjective welfare and how they may be affected by comparing oneself with others; and (c) the role of empathy in influencing moral feeling.[4]

Now it should be obvious that if racism is as central to the polity as I have argued, then it will have a major shaping effect on white cognizers in all these areas. (a) Because of the intellectual atmosphere produced by the Racial Contract, whites will (in phase one) take for granted the appropriateness of concepts *legitimizing* the racial order, privileging them as the master race and relegating nonwhites to subpersonhood, and later (in phase two) the appropriateness of concepts that *derace* the polity, denying its actual racial structuring.[5] (b) Because of the reciprocally dependent definitions of superior whiteness and inferior nonwhiteness, whites may consciously or unconsciously assess how they're doing by a scale that depends in part on how nonwhites are doing, since the essence of whiteness is entitlement to differential privilege vis-à-vis nonwhites as a whole.[6] (c) Because the Racial Contract requires the exploitation of nonwhites, it requires in whites the cultivation of patterns of affect and empathy that are only weakly, if at all, influenced by nonwhite suffering. In all three cases, then, there are interesting structures of moral cognitive distortion that could be linked to race, and one hopes that this new research program will be exploring some of them (though the past record of neglect does not give any great reason for optimism).

This partitioned moral concern can usefully be thought of as a kind of *"Herrenvolk* ethics,"* with the principles applicable to the white subset (the humans) mutating suitably as they cross the color line to the nonwhite subset (the less-than-humans). (Susan Opotow has done a detailed study of moralities of exclusion, in which certain "individuals or groups are perceived as outside the boundary in which moral values, rules, and considerations of fairness apply"; so this would be a racial version of such a morality.)[7] One could then generate, variously, a *Herrenvolk* Lockeanism, where whiteness itself becomes property, nonwhites do not fully, or at all, own themselves, and nonwhite labor does not appropriate nature;[8] a *Herrenvolk* Kantianism, where nonwhites count as subpersons of considerably less than infinite value, required to give racial deference rather than equal respect to white persons, and white self-respect, correspondingly, is conceptually tied to this nonwhite deference;[9] and a *Herrenvolk* utilitarianism, where nonwhites count distributively for less than one and are deemed to suffer less acutely than whites.[10] The actual details of the basic values of the particular normative theory (property rights, personhood and respect, welfare) are not important, since *all* theories can be appropriately adjusted internally to bring about the desired outcome: what is crucial is the theorist's adherence to the Racial Contract.

Being its primary victims, nonwhites have, of course, always been aware of this peculiar schism running through the white psyche. Many years ago, in his classic novel *Invisible Man*, Ralph Ellison had his nameless black narrator point out that whites must have a peculiar reciprocal "construction of [their] *inner* eyes" which renders black Americans invisible, since they "refuse to see me." The Racial Contract includes an epistemological contract, an epistemology of ignorance. "Recognition is a form of agreement," and by the terms of the Racial Contract, whites have agreed not to recognize blacks as equal persons. Thus the white pedestrian who bumps into the black narrator at the start is a representative figure, somebody "lost in a dream world." "But didn't *he* control that dream world—which, alas, is only too real!—and didn't *he* rule me out of it? And if he had yelled for a policeman, wouldn't *I* have been taken for the offending one? Yes, yes, yes!"[11] Similarly, James Baldwin argues that white supremacy "forced [white] Americans into rationalizations so fantastic that they approached the pathological," generating a tortured ignorance so structured that one cannot raise certain issues with whites "because even if I should speak, no one would believe me," and paradoxically, "they would not believe me precisely because they would know that what I said was true."[12]

Evasion and self-deception thus become the epistemic norm. Describing America's "national web of self-deceptions" on race, Richard Drinnon cites as an explanation Montesquieu's wry observation about African enslavement: "It is impossible for us to suppose these creatures to be men, because, allowing them to be men, a suspicion would follow that we ourselves are not Christians." The founding ideology of the white settler state required the conceptual erasure of those societies that had been there before: "For [a writer of the time] to have consistently regarded Indians as persons with a psychology of their own would have upended his world. It would have meant recognizing that 'the state of nature' really had full-fledged people in it and that both it and the cherished 'civil society' had started out as lethal figments of the European imagination."[13] An Australian historian comments likewise on the existence of "something like a cult of forgetfulness practised on a national scale" with respect to Aborigines.[14] Lewis Gordon, working in the existential phenomenological tradition, draws on Sartrean notions to argue that in a world structured around race, bad faith necessarily becomes pervasive: "In bad faith, I flee a displeasing truth for a pleasing falsehood. I must convince myself that a falsehood is in fact true. . . . Under the model of bad faith, the stubborn racist has made a choice not to admit certain uncomfortable truths about his group and chooses not to challenge certain comfortable falsehoods about other people. . . . Since he has made this choice, he will resist whatever threatens it. . . . The more the racist plays the game of evasion, the more estranged he will make himself from his 'inferiors' and the more he will sink into the world that is required to maintain this evasion."[15] In the ideal polity one seeks to know oneself and to know the world; here such knowledge may be dangerous.

Correspondingly, the Racial Contract also explains the actual astonishing historical record of European atrocity against nonwhites, which quantitatively and qualitatively, in numbers and horrific detail, cumulatively dwarfs all other kinds of ethnically/racially motivated massacres put together: *la leyenda negra*—the black legend—of Spanish colonialism, defamatory only in its invidious singling out of the Spanish, since it would later be emulated by Spain's envious competitors, the Dutch, French, and English, seeking to create legends of their own; the killing through mass murder and disease of 95 percent of the indigenous population of the Americas, with recent revisionist scholarship, as mentioned, having dramatically increased the estimates of the preconquest population, so that— at roughly 100 million victims—this would easily rank as the single greatest act of genocide in human history;[16] the infamous slogans, now somewhat embarrassing to a generation living under a different phase of the Contract—"Kill the nits, and you'll have no lice!" as American cavalryman John House advised when he shot a Sauk infant at the Wisconsin Bad Axe massacre,[17] and "The only good injun is a dead injun"; the slow-motion Holocaust of African slavery, which is now estimated by some to have claimed thirty to sixty million lives in Africa, the Middle Passage, and the "seasoning" process, even before the degradation and destruction of slave life in the Americas;[18] the casual acceptance as no crime, just the necessary clearing of the territory of pestilential "varmints" and "critters," of the random killing of stray Indians in America or Aborigines in Australia or Bushmen in South Africa; the massively punitive European colonial retaliations after native uprisings; the death toll from the direct and indirect consequences of the forced labor of the colonial economies, such as the millions (original estimates as high as ten million) who died in the Belgian Congo as a result of Leopold II's quest for rubber, though strangely it is to Congolese rather than European savagery that a "heart of darkness" is attributed;[19] the appropriation of the nonwhite body, not merely metaphorically (as the black body can be said to have been consumed on the slave plantations to produce European capital), but *literally*, whether as utilitarian tool or as war trophy. As utilitarian tools, Native Americans were occasionally skinned and made into bridle reins (for example by U.S. President Andrew Jackson),[20] Tasmanians were killed and used as dog meat,[21] and in World War II Jewish hair was made into cushions, and (not as well known) Japanese bones were made by some Americans into letter openers. As war trophies, Indian scalps, Vietnamese ears, and Japanese ears, gold teeth, and skulls were all collected (*Life* magazine carried a photograph of a Japanese skull being used as a hood ornament on a U.S. military vehicle, and some soldiers sent skulls home as presents for their girlfriends).[22] To these we can add the fact that because of the penal reforms advocated by Cesare Beccaria and others, torture was more or less eliminated in Europe by the end of the eighteenth century, while it continued to be routinely practiced in the colonies and on the slave plantations—whippings, castrations, dismemberments, roastings over slow fires, being smeared with sugar, buried up to the neck, and then left for the insects to devour, being filled with gunpowder and then blown up, and so on;[23] the fact that in America the medieval tradition of the auto-da-fé, the public burning, survived well into the twentieth century, with thousands of spectators sometimes gathering for the festive occasion of the southern barbecue, bringing children, picnic baskets, etc., and subsequently fighting over the remains to see who could get the toes or the knucklebones before adjourning to a celebratory dance in the evening;[24] the fact that the rules of war at least theoretically regulating intra-European combat were abandoned or suspended for non-Europeans, so that by papal edict the use of the crossbow was initially forbidden against Christians but permitted against Islam, the dum-dum (hollow-point) bullet was originally prohibited within Europe but used in the colonial wars,[25] the machine gun was brought to perfection in the late nineteenth century in subjugating Africans armed usually only with spears or a few obsolete firearms, so that in the glorious 1898 British victory over the Sudanese at Omdurman, for example, eleven thousand black warriors were killed at the cost of forty-eight British soldiers, a long-distance massacre in which no Sudanese "got closer than three hundred yards from the British positions,"[26] the atomic bomb was used not once but twice against the civilian population of a yellow people at a time when military necessity could only questionably be cited (causing Justice Radhabinod Pal, in his dissenting opinion in the Tokyo War Crimes Trials, to argue that Allied leaders should have been put on trial with the Japanese).[27] We can mention the six million Jews killed in the camps and ghettos of Europe and the millions of members of other "inferior" races (Romani, Slavs) killed there and by the *Einsatzgruppen* on the Eastern Front by the Nazi rewriting of the Racial Contract to make them too nonwhites;[28] the pattern of unpunished rape, torture, and massacre in the twentieth-century colonial/neocolonial and in part racial wars of Algeria (during the course of which about one million Algerians, or one-tenth of the country's population, perished) and Vietnam, illustrated by the fact that Lieutenant William Calley was the only American convicted of war crimes in Vietnam and, for his role in directing the mass murder of five hundred women, children, and old men (or, more cautiously and qualifiedly, "Oriental human beings," as the deposition put it), was sentenced to life at hard labor but had his sentence quickly commuted by presidential intervention to "house arrest" at his Fort Benning bachelor apartment, where he remained for three years before being freed on parole, then and now doubtless a bit puzzled by the fuss, since, as he told the military psychiatrists examining him, "he did not feel as if he were killing humans but rather that they were animals with whom one could not speak or reason."[29]

For these and many other horrors too numerous to list, the ideal Kantian (social contract) norm of the infinite value of all human life thus has to be rewritten to reflect the actual (Racial Contract) norm of the far greater value of *white* life, and the corresponding crystallization of feelings of vastly differential outrage over white and nonwhite death, white and nonwhite suffering. If looking back (or sometimes just looking across), one wants to ask "But how could they?" the answer is that it is easy once a certain social ontology has been created. Bewilderment and puzzlement show that one is taking for granted the morality of the literal social contract as a norm; once one begins from the Racial Contract, the mystery evaporates. The Racial Contract thus makes White moral psychology transparent; one is not continually being "surprised" when one examines the historical record, because this is the psychology the contract prescribes. (The theory of the Racial Contract is not *cynical*, because cynicism really implies theoretical breakdown, a despairing throwing up of the hands and a renunciation of the project of understanding the world and human evil for a mystified yearning for a prelapsarian man. The "Racial Contract" is simply *realist*—willing to look at the facts without flinching, to explain that if you start with *this*, then you will end up with *that*.)

Similarly, the "Racial Contract" makes the Jewish Holocaust—misleadingly designated as *the* Holocaust—comprehensible, distancing itself theoretically both from positions that would render it cognitively opaque, inexplicably sui generis, and from positions that would downplay the racial dimension and assimilate it to the undifferentiated terrorism of German fascism. From the clouded perspective of the Third World, the question in Arno Mayer's title *Why Did the Heavens Not Darken?* betrays a climatic Eurocentrism, which fails to recognize that the blue skies were only smiling on *Europe*. The influential view he cites (not his own) is typical: "Prima facie the catastrophe which befell the Jews during the Second World War was unique in its own time and unprecedented in history. There are strong reasons to believe that the victimization of the Jews was so enormous and atrocious as to be completely outside the bounds of all other human experience. If that is the case, what the Jews were subjected to will forever defy historical reconstruction and interpretation, let alone comprehension."[30] But this represents an astonishing white amnesia about the actual historical record. Likewise, the despairing question of how there can be poetry after Auschwitz evokes the puzzled nonwhite reply of how there could have been poetry *before* Auschwitz, and *after* the killing fields in America, Africa, Asia. The standpoint of Native America, black Africa, colonial Asia, has always been aware that European civilization rests on extra-European barbarism, so that the Jewish Holocaust, the "Judeocide" (Mayer), is by no means a bolt from the blue, an unfathomable anomaly in the development of the West, but unique only in that it represents use of the Racial Contract against *Europeans*. I say this in no way to diminish its horror, of course, but rather to deny its *singularity*, to establish its conceptual identity with other policies carried out by Europe in non-Europe for hundreds of years, but using methods less efficient than those made possible by advanced mid-twentieth-century industrial society.

In the twilight world of the Cold War, the term "blowback" was used in American spy jargon to refer to "unexpected—and negative—effects at home that result from covert operations overseas," particularly from (what were called) "black" operations of assassination and government overthrow.[31] A case can be made for seeing the "blowback" from the overseas ("white") operations of European conquest, settlement, slavery, and colonialism as consolidating in the modern European mind a racialized ethic that, in combination with traditional anti-Semitism, eventually boomeranged, returning to Europe itself to facilitate the Jewish Holocaust. Forty years ago, in his classic polemic *Discourse on Colonialism*, Aimé Césaire pointed out the implicit double standard in European "outrage" at Nazism: "It is Nazism, yes, but . . . before [Europeans] were its victims, they were its accomplices; that they tolerated that Nazism before it was inflicted on them, that they absolved it, shut their eyes to it, legitimized it, because, until then, it had been applied only to non-European peoples. . . . [Hitler's crime is] the fact that he applied to Europe colonialist procedures which until then had been reserved exclusively for the Arabs of Algeria, the coolies of India, and the blacks of Africa."[32] The Racial Contract continues, with a truly grisly irony, to manifest itself even in the *condemnation* of the consequences of the Racial Contract, since the racial mass murder of Europeans is placed on a different moral plane than the racial mass murder of non-Europeans. Similarly, Kiernan argues that King Leopold's Congo "cast before it the shadow that was to turn into Hitler's empire inside Europe. . . . Attitudes acquired during the subjugation of the other continents now reproduced themselves at home."[33] So in this explanatory framework, unlike the subsumption of the death camps under a deraced fascism, the racial dimension and the establishment of Jewish nonwhite subpersonhood *are* explanatorily crucial. If, as earlier argued, the Jews were by this time basically "off-white" rather than "nonwhite," assimilated into the population of persons, the Nazis could be said to be in local violation of the global Racial Contract by excluding from the club of Whiteness groups already grudgingly admitted, by doing to Europeans (even borderline ones) what (by then) was only supposed to be done to non-Europeans.

Postwar writings on this subject by Europeans, both in Europe and in North America, have generally sought to block these conceptual connections, representing Nazi policy as more deviant than it actually was, for example, in the *Historikerstreit*, the German debate over the uniqueness of the Jewish Holocaust. The dark historical record of European imperialism has been forgotten. Robert Harris's chilling 1992 novel *Fatherland*, a classic in the alternative-worlds science fiction genre, depicts a future in which the Nazis have won World War II and have eradicated from the record their killing of the Jews, so that only scattered evidence survives.[34] But in certain respects we live in an actual, nonalternative world where the victors of racial killing really *did* win and have reconstructed and falsified the record accordingly. Holocaust denial and Holocaust apologia thus long precede the post-1945 period, going back all the way to the original response to the revelations of Las Casas's *Devastation of the Indies* in 1542.[35] Yet, with few exceptions, only recently has revisionist white historiography belatedly begun to catch up with this nonwhite conceptualization—hence the title of David Stannard's book on the Columbian conquest, *American Holocaust*; the related title of an anthology (cited by Noam Chomsky in his *Year 501*) put out in Germany in anticipation of the quincentenary, *Das Fünfhundert-jährige Reich* (Five-hundred year reich); and the Swedish writer Sven Lindqvist's recently translated *"Exterminate All the Brutes,"* which explicitly links the famous injunction of Conrad's Kurtz to Nazi practice: "Auschwitz was the modern industrial application of a policy of extermination on which European world domination had long since rested. . . . And when what had been done in the heart of darkness was repeated in the heart of Europe, no one recognized it. No one wished to admit what everyone knew. . . . It is not knowledge we lack. What is missing is the courage to understand what we know and draw conclusions."[36]

The debate will doubtless continue for many decades to come. But on a closing note, it does not seem inappropriate to get the opinion of that well-known moral and political theorist Adolf Hitler (surely a man with something worthwhile to say on the subject), who, looking ahead in a 1932 speech, "explicitly located his *Lebensraum* project within the long trajectory of European racial conquest."[37] As he explained to his presumably attentive audience, you cannot understand "the economically privileged supremacy of the white race over the rest of the world" except by relating it to "a political concept of supremacy which has been peculiar to the white race as a natural phenomenon for many centuries and which it has upheld as such to the outer world":

> Take for example India: England did not acquire India in a lawful and legitimate manner, but rather without regard to the natives' wishes, views, or declarations of rights. . . . Just as Cortes or Pizarro demanded for themselves Central America and the northern states of South America not on the basis of any legal claim, but from the absolute, inborn feeling of superiority of the white race. The settlement of the North American continent was similarly a consequence not of any higher claim in a democratic or international sense, but rather of a consciousness of what is right which had its sole roots in the conviction of the superiority and thus the right of the white race.

So his plan was just to uphold this inspiring Western tradition, this racial "right to dominate (*Herrenrecht*)," this "frame of mind . . . which has conquered the world" for the white race, since "from this political view there evolved the basis for the economic takeover of the rest of the world."[38] In other words, he saw himself as simply doing at home what his fellow Europeans had long been doing abroad.

Finally, the theory of the Racial Contract, by separating whiteness as phenotype/racial classification from Whiteness as a politicoeconomic system committed to white supremacy, opens a theoretical space for white *repudiation* of the Contract. (One could then distinguish "being white" from "being White.")

There is an interesting point of contrast here with the social contract. One obvious early objection to the notion of society's being based on a "contract" was that even if an original founding contract had existed, it wouldn't bind later generations, who hadn't signed it. There have been various attempts by contractarians to get around this problem, the best-known being Locke's notion of "tacit consent."[39] The idea is that if you choose as an adult to stay in your country of birth and make use of its benefits, then you have "tacitly" consented to obey the government and thus to be bound by the contract. But David Hume is famously scathing about this claim, saying that the notion of tacit consent is vacuous where there is no real possibility of opting out by moving to a no-longer-existent state of nature or of being able to emigrate when you have no particular skills and no other language but your mother tongue.[40] You stay because you have no real choice.

But for the Racial Contract, it is different. There *is* a real choice for whites, though admittedly a difficult one. The rejection of the Racial Contract and the normed inequities of the white polity does not require one to leave the country but to speak out and struggle against the terms of the Contract. So in this case, moral/political judgments about one's "consent" to the legitimacy of the political system and conclusions about one's effectively having become a signatory to the "contract," *are* apropos—and so are judgments of one's culpability. By unquestioningly "going along with things," by accepting all the privileges of whiteness with concomitant complicity in the system of white supremacy, one can be said to have consented to Whiteness.

And in fact there have always been praiseworthy whites—anticolonialists, abolitionists, opponents of imperialism, civil rights activists, resisters of apartheid—who have recognized the existence and immorality of Whiteness as a political system, challenged its legitimacy, and insofar as possible, refused the Contract. (Inasmuch as mere skin color will automatically continue to privilege them, of course, this identification with the oppressed can usually be only partial.) Thus the interesting moral/political phenomenon of the *white renegade*, the *race traitor* in the language of the Klan (accurate enough insofar as "race" here denotes Whiteness),[41] the colonial explorer who "goes native," the soldier in French Indochina who contracts *le mal jaune*, the yellow disorder (the perilous illness of "attachment . . . to Indochina's landscape, people . . . and culture"),[42] the nigger-, Injun-, or Jew-lover. These individuals betray the white polity in the name of a broader definition of the polis—"Treason to whiteness is loyalty to humanity"[43]— thus becoming "renegades from the States, traitors to their country and to civilization," "a white Injun, and there's nothing more despicable."[44] For as the term signifies, where morality has been racialized, the practice of a genuinely color-blind ethic requires the repudiation of one's *Herrenvolk* standing and its accompanying moral epistemology, thus eliciting the appropriate moral condemnation from the race loyalists and white signatories who have not repudiated either.

The level of commitment and sacrifice will, of course, vary. Some have written exposés of the hidden truth of the Racial Contract—Las Casas's *Devastation of the Indies:* abolitionist literature; the French writer Abbé Raynal's call for black slave revolution; Mark Twain's writings for the Anti–Imperialist League (usually suppressed as an embarrassment by his biographers, as Chomsky notes);[45] Sartre and Simone de Beauvoir's principled oppositional journalism against their country's colonial war. Some have tried to save some of its victims—the Underground Railroad; Aborigines Protection Societies; Oskar Schindler's Jewish charges; Don Macleod, the Australian white man "accepted as an honorary Aborigine, who helped organize the first Aboriginal strike in the Pilbara in 1946";[46] Hugh Thompson, the American helicopter pilot who threatened to fire on his fellow soldiers unless they stopped massacring Vietnamese civilians at My Lai.[47] Some have actually given their lives for the struggle—the white American antislavery revolutionary John Brown; the white members of the African National Congress who died trying to abolish apartheid. But the mere fact of their existence shows what was possible, throwing into contrast and rendering open for moral judgment the behavior of their fellow whites, who chose to accept Whiteness instead.

The Racial Contract has always been recognized by nonwhites as the real determinant of (most) white moral/political practice and thus as the real moral/political agreement to be challenged.

If the epistemology of the signatories, the agents, of the Racial Contract requires evasion and denial of the realities of race, the epistemology of the victims, the objects, of the Racial Contract is, unsurprisingly, focused on these realities themselves. (So there is a reciprocal relationship, the Racial Contract tracking white moral/political consciousness, the reaction to the Racial Contract tracking nonwhite moral/political consciousness and stimulating a puzzled investigation *of* that white moral/political consciousness.) The term "standpoint theory" is now routinely used to signify the notion that in understanding the workings of a system of oppression, a perspective from the bottom up is more likely to be accurate than one from the top down. What is involved here, then, is a "racial" version of standpoint theory, a perspectival cognitive advantage that is grounded in the phenomenological experience of the disjuncture between official (white) reality and actual (nonwhite) experience, the "double-consciousness" of which W. E. B. Du Bois spoke.[48] This differential racial experience generates an alternative moral and political perception of social reality which is encapsulated in the insight from the black American folk tradition I have used as the epigraph of this book: the central realization, summing up the Racial Contract, that "when white people say 'Justice,' they mean 'Just Us.'"

Nonwhites have always (at least in first encounters) been bemused or astonished by the *invisibility* of the Racial Contract to whites, the fact that whites have routinely talked in universalist terms even when it has been quite clear that the scope has really been limited to themselves. Correspondingly, nonwhites, with no vested material or psychic interest in the Racial Contract—objects rather than subjects of it, viewing it from outside rather than inside, subpersons rather than persons—are (at least before ideological conditioning) able to see its terms quite clearly. Thus the hypocrisy of the racial polity is most transparent to its victims. The corollary is that nonwhite interest in white moral and political theory has necessarily been focused less on the details of the particular competing moral and political candidates (utilitarianism versus deontology versus natural rights theory; liberalism versus conservatism versus socialism) than in the unacknowledged Racial Contract that has usually framed their functioning. The variable that makes the most difference to the fate of nonwhites is not the fine- or even coarse-grained conceptual divergences of the different theories themselves (all have their *Herrenvolk* variants), but *whether or not the subclause invoking the Racial Contract, thus putting the theory into* Herrenvolk *mode, has been activated.* The details of the moral theories thus become less important than the *meta*theory, the Racial Contract, in which they are embedded. The crucial question is whether nonwhites are counted as full persons, part of the population covered by the moral operator, or not.

The preoccupation of nonwhite moral and political thought with issues of *race*, puzzling alike to a white liberalism predicated on colorless atomic individuals and a white Marxism predicated on colorless classes in struggle, thus becomes readily explicable once the reality of the Racial Contract has been conceded. What is involved is neither a simple variant of traditional European nationalism (to which it is sometimes assimilated) nor a mysterious political project unfolding in some alien theoretical space (as in the mutually opaque language games postulated by postmodernism). The unifying conceptual space within which *both* orthodox white moral/political philosophy *and* unorthodox nonwhite moral/political philosophy are developing is the space that locates the (mythical) social contract on the same plane as the (real) Racial Contract, being predicated on the translation of "race" into the mutually commensurable and mutually intelligible language of personhood, and thereby demonstrating that these are contiguous, indeed *identical*, spaces—not so much a *different* conceptual universe as a recognition of the dark matter of the *existing* one. Personhood can be taken for granted by some, while it (and all that accompanies it) has to be fought for by others, so that the general human political project of struggling for a better society involves a different trajectory for nonwhites.

It is no accident, then, that the moral and political theory and practical struggles of nonwhites have so often centered on race, the marker of personhood and subpersonhood, inclusion within or exclusion from the racial polity. The formal contractarian apparatus I have tried to develop will not be articulated as such. But the crucial notions of the *person/subperson* differentiation, the correspondingly racially structured moral code (*Herrenvolk* ethics), and the *white-supremacist character* of the polity can be found in one form or another everywhere in Native American, black American, and Third and Fourth World anticolonial thought.

Sitting Bull asks: "What treaty that the whites have kept

has the red man broken? Not one. What treaty that the white man ever made with us have they kept? Not one. When I was a boy the Sioux owned the world; the sun rose and set on their land. . . . Where are our lands? Who owns them? What white man can say I ever stole his land or a penny of his money? Yet, they say I am a thief. . . . What law have I broken? Is it wrong for me to love my own? Is it wicked for me because my skin is red?" Ward Churchill, another Native American, characterizes European settlers as a self-conceived "master race." David Walker complains that whites consider blacks "not of the human family," forcing blacks "to prove to them ourselves, that we are MEN." W. E. B. Du Bois represents blacks as a "tertium quid," "somewhere between men and cattle," comments that "Liberty, Justice, and Right" are marked "'For White People Only,'" and suggests that "the statement 'I am white'" is becoming "the one fundamental tenet of our practical morality." Richard Wright analyzes "the ethics of living Jim Crow." Marcus Garvey concludes that blacks are "a race without respect." Jawaharlal Nehru claims that British policy in India is "that of the herrenvolk and the master race." Martin Luther King Jr. describes the feeling of "forever fighting a degenerating sense of 'nobodiness.'" Malcolm X asserts that America "has not only deprived us of the right to be a citizen, she has deprived us of the right to be human beings, the right to be recognized and respected as men and women. . . . We are fighting for recognition as human beings." Frantz Fanon maps a colonial world divided between "two different species," a "governing race" and "zoological" natives. Aimé Césaire argues that "the colonizer . . . in order to ease his conscience gets into the habit of seeing the other man as an animal. . . . colonization = 'thingification.'" Australian Aborigines in a 1982 protest statement at the Commonwealth Games in Brisbane point out that "since the White invasion . . . [o]ur humanity is being degraded and our history distorted by strangers. . . . Before the World, we accuse White Australia (and her Mother, England) of crimes against humanity and the planet. The past two centuries of colonisation is proof of our accusation. *We hereby demand yet again recognition of our humanity and our land rights.*"[49] The central moral commonality uniting all their experiences is the reality of racial subordination, necessarily generating a different moral topography from the one standardly examined in white ethical discourse.

Correspondingly, the polity was usually thought of in racial terms, as white ruled, and this perspective would become global in the period of formal colonial administration. Political theory is in part about who the main actors are, and for this unacknowledged polity they are neither the atomic individuals of classic liberal thought nor the classes of Marxist theory but races. The various native and colonial peoples' attempts (usually unsuccessful, too little and too late) to forge a *racial* unity—Pan-Indianism, Pan-Africanism, Pan-Arabism, Pan-Asianism, Pan-Islamism—arose in response to an *already achieved* white unity, a Pan-Europeanism formalized and incorporated by the terms of the Racial Contract.

In the period of de jure global white supremacy, of colonialism and slavery, this solidarity was clearly perceived by whites also. "That race is everything, is simply a fact," writes Scotsman Robert Knox in *The Races of Men* (1850),[50] and theories of the necessity of racial struggle, race war, against the subordinate races are put forward as obvious. Darwin's work raised hopes in some quarters that natural selection (perhaps with a little help from its friends) would sweep away the remaining inferior races, as it had already done so providentially in the Americas and Tasmania, so that the planet as a whole could be cleared for white settlement.[51] And after that only the sky would be the limit. In fact, even the sky would *not* be the limit, for there was always the solar system. Cecil Rhodes dreamed that perhaps he could "annex the planets" for Britain: "Where there is space, there is hope."[52]

But alas, this noble dream was not to be realized. Even with encouragement, nonwhites did not die fast enough. So whites had to settle for colonial rule over stubbornly growing native populations, while of course keeping a watchful eye out for both rebellion and subversive notions of self-government. Witness the various colored perils—red (Native American, that is), black, and yellow—that have haunted the European and Euro-implanted imagination. "Europe," Kiernan comments, "thought of its identity in terms of race or color and plagued itself with fears of the Yellow Peril or a Black Peril—boomerang effects, as they might be called, of a White Peril from which the other continents were more tangibly suffering."[53] The political framework is quite explicitly predicated on the notion that whites everywhere have a common interest in maintaining global white supremacy against insurrections conceived of in racial terms. At the turn of the century, Europeans were worried about the "vast ant-heap" filled with "soldier-ants" of China, while "similar fears were in the air about a huge black army," threatening a race war of revenge led by "dusky Napoleons."[54]

Though there were occasional breaches for strategic national advantage, international white racial solidarity was generally demonstrated in the joint actions to suppress and isolate slave rebellions and colonial uprisings: the boycott of Haiti, the only successful slave revolution in history (and, noncoincidentally, today the poorest country in the Western Hemisphere), the common intervention against the 1899–1900 Boxer rebellion in China, the concern raised by the 1905 Japanese victory over Russia. As late as the early twentieth century, books were still being published with such warning titles as *The Passing of* the Great Race and The Rising Tide of Color against White World-Supremacy.[55] Intra-European differences and conflicts were real enough but would be quickly put aside in the face of the nonwhite threat: "In the course of their rivalries Europeans exchanged many hard words, and sometimes abused each other in order to please a non-European people. . . . But when it came to any serious colonial upheaval, white men felt their kinship, and Europe drew together. . . . Above all, and very remarkably, despite innumerable crises over rival claims the European countries managed from the War of American Independence onward to avoid a single colonial war among themselves."[56]

This unity ended in the twentieth century with the outbreak of World War I, which was in part an interimperialist war over competing colonial claims. But despite nonwhite agitation and military participation (largely as cannon fodder) in the armies of their respective mother countries, the postwar settlement led not to decolonization but to a territorial redistribution among the colonial powers themselves. ("OK, I'll take this one, and you can take that one.") In the interwar years Japan's Pan-Asiatic Greater East Asia Co-Prosperity Sphere was seen by most white Western leaders as a threat to global white supremacy. Indeed, as late as World War II, the popular American writer Pearl Buck had to warn her readers that colonized peoples would not continue to put up with global white domination, and that unless there was change their discontent would lead to "the longest of human wars . . . the war between the white man and his world and the colored man and his world."[57]

Corresponding to this global white solidarity transcending national boundaries, the virtual white polity, nonwhites' common interest in abolishing the Racial Contract manifested itself in patterns of partisan emotional identification which from a modern, more nationalistic perspective now seem quite bizarre. In 1879, for example, when the King of Burma learned of the Zulu defeat of a British army at Isandhlwana, he immediately announced his intention of marching on Rangoon.[58] In 1905 Indians cheered the Japanese victory over the czar's (white) armies in the Russo-Japanese war.[59] In the Spanish-American War, black Americans raised doubts about the point of being "a black man in the army of the white man sent to kill the brown man," and a few blacks actually went over to the side of Emilio Aguinaldo's Filipino forces.[60] After Pearl Harbor, the ominous joke circulated in the American press of a black sharecropper who comments to his white boss, "By the way, Captain, I hear the Japs done declared war on you white folks"; black civil rights militants demanded the "double-victory," "Victory at Home as Well as Abroad"; Japanese intelligence considered the possibility of an alliance with black Americans in a domestic colored front against white supremacy; and white Americans worried about black loyalty.[61] The 1954 Vietnamese victory over the French at Dien Bien Phu (like the Japanese capture of Singapore in World War II) was in part seen as a *racial* triumph, the defeat of a white by a brown people, a blow against the arrogance of global white supremacy.

So on the level of the popular consciousness of nonwhites—particularly in the first phase of the Racial Contract, but lingering on into the second phase—racial self-identification was deeply embedded, with the notion that nonwhites everywhere were engaged in some kind of common political struggle, so that a victory for one was a victory for all. The different battles around the world against slavery, colonialism, jim crow, the "color bar," European imperialism, apartheid were in a sense all part of a common struggle against the Racial Contract. As Gary Okihiro points out, what came into existence was "a global racial formation that complemented and buttressed the economic and political world-system," thus generating "trans-national identities of white and nonwhite."[62] It is this world—this moral and political reality—that W. E. B. Du Bois was describing in his famous 1900 Pan-Africanist statement "To the Nations of the World": "The problem of the twentieth century is the problem of the color line," since, as he would later point out, too many have accepted "that tacit but clear modern philosophy which assigns to the white race alone the hegemony of the world and assumes that other races . . . will either be content to serve the interests of the whites or die out before their all-conquering march."[63] It is this world that later produced the 1955 Bandung (Indonesia) Conference, a meeting of twenty-nine Asian and African nations, the "under-dogs of the human race" in Richard Wright's phrase, whose decision to discuss "racialism and colonialism" caused such consternation in the West at the time,[64] the meeting that even-tually led to the formation of the Non-Aligned Movement. And it is this world that stimulated, in 1975, the creation of the World Council of Indigenous Peoples, uniting Australian Aborigines, New Zealand Maoris, and American Indians.[65]

If to white readers this intellectual world, only half a century distant, now seems like a universe of alien concepts, it is a tribute to the success of the rewritten Racial Contract in transforming the terms of public discourse so that white domi-nation is now conceptually invisible. As Leon Poliakov points out, the embarrassment of the death camps (on European soil, anyway) led the postwar European intelligentsia to a sanitiza-tion of the past record, in which racism became the aberrant invention of scapegoat figures such as Joseph-Arthur Gobi-neau: "A vast chapter of western thought is thus made to disappear by sleight of hand, and this conjuring trick corre-sponds, on the psychological or psycho-historical level, to the collective suppression of troubling memories and embarrassing truths."[66] That the revival of Anglo-American political philosophy takes place in *this* period, the present epoch of the de facto Racial Contract, partially explains its otherworldly race insensitivity. The history of imperialism, colonialism, and genocide, the reality of systemic racial exclusion, are obfuscated in seemingly abstract and general categories that originally were restricted to white citizens.

But the overtly political battles—for emancipation, decolonization, civil rights, land rights—were only part of this struggle. The terms of the Racial Contract norm nonwhite persons themselves, establishing morally, epistemically, and aesthetically their ontological inferiority. To the extent that nonwhites accept this, to the extent that *they* also were signatories to the Contract, there is a corollary personal dimension to this struggle which is accommodated with difficulty, if at all, in the categories of mainstream political philosophy. Operating on the terrain of the social contract and thus taking personhood for granted, failing to recognize the reality of the Racial Contract, orthodox political theory has difficulty making sense of the multidimensionality of oppositional nonwhite political thought.

What does it require for a subperson to assert himself or herself politically? To begin with, it means simply, or not so simply, claiming the moral status of personhood. So it means challenging the white-constructed ontology that has deemed one a "body impolitic," an entity not entitled to assert personhood in the first place. In a sense one has to fight an internal battle before even advancing onto the ground of external combat. One has to overcome the internalization of subpersonhood prescribed by the Racial Contract and recognize one's own humanity, resisting the official category of despised aboriginal, natural slave, colonial ward. One has to learn the basic self-respect that can casually be assumed by Kantian persons, those privileged by the Racial Contract, but which is denied to subpersons. Particularly for blacks, ex-slaves, the importance of developing self-respect and demanding respect from whites is crucial. Frederick Douglass recounts "how a man was made a slave," and promises "you shall see how a slave was made a man."[67] But a hundred years later this struggle is still in progress. "*Negroes want to be treated like men*," wrote James Baldwin in the 1950s, "a perfectly straightforward statement, containing only seven words. People who have mastered Kant, Hegel, Shakespeare, Marx, Freud, and the Bible find this statement utterly impenetrable."[68]

Linked with this personal struggle will be an epistemic dimension, cognitive resistance to the racially mystificatory aspects of white theory, the painstaking reconstruction of past and present necessary to fill in the crucial gaps and erase the slanders of the globally dominant European worldview. One has to learn to trust one's own cognitive powers, to develop one's own concepts, insights, modes of explanation, overarching theories, and to oppose the epistemic hegemony of conceptual frameworks designed in part to thwart and suppress the exploration of such matters; one has to think *against the grain.* There are excavations of the histories concealed by the Racial Contract: Native American, black American, African and Asian and Pacific investigation and valorization of their pasts, giving the lie to the description of "savagery" and state-of-nature existence of "peoples without history."[69] The exposure of the misrepresentations of Eurocentrism, not-so-innocent "white lies" and "white mythologies," is thus part of the political project of reclaiming personhood.[70] The long history of what has been called, in the black oppositional tradition, "vindicationist" scholarship,[71] is a necessary political response to the fabrications of the Racial Contract, which has no correlate in the political theory of the *social* contract because Europeans were in cultural control of their own past and, so, could be confident it would not be misrepresented (or, perhaps better, that the misrepresentations would be their own).

Finally, the *somatic* aspect of the Racial Contract—the necessary reference it makes to the body—explains the *body politics* that nonwhites have often incorporated into their struggle. Global white supremacy denies subpersons not merely moral and cognitive but also aesthetic parity. Particularly for the black body, phenotypically most distant from the Caucasoid somatic norm, the implications often are the attempt to transform oneself as far as possible into an imitation of the white body.[72] Thus the assertion of full black personhood has also sometimes manifested itself in the self-conscious repudiation of somatic transformation and the proclamation "Black is beautiful!" For mainstream political philosophy this is merely a fashion statement; for a theory informed by the Racial Contract, it is part of the political project of reclaiming personhood.

The "Racial Contract" as a theory is explanatorily superior to the raceless social contract in accounting for the political and moral realities of the world and in helping to guide normative theory.

The "Racial Contract" as a naturalized account (henceforth simply the "Racial Contract") is theoretically superior to the raceless social contract as a model of the actual world and, correspondingly, of what needs to be done to reform it. I therefore advocate the supplementation of standard social contract discussions with an account of the "Racial Contract."

It might be replied that I am making a kind of "category mistake," since even if my claims about the centrality of racism to recent global history are true, modern contractarianism has long since *given up* real-world explanatory pretensions, being hypothetical, subjunctive exercises in *ideal* theory. So the fact that actual societies were not based on these norms, even if true, and unfortunate, is simply irrelevant. These are just two different kinds of projects.

The discussion at the beginning should have made clear why I think this answer misses the point. Insofar as the moral theory and political philosophy of present-day contractarianism are trying to prescribe ideals for a just society, which are presumably intended to help transform our present *non*ideal society, it is obviously important to get clear what the facts are. Moral and political prescription will depend in part on empirical claims and theoretical generalizations, accounts of what happened in the past and what is happening now, as well as more abstract views about how society and the state work and where political power is located. If the facts are radically different from those that are conventionally represented, the prescriptions are also likely to be radically different.

Now as I pointed out at the start, and indeed throughout, the absence from most white moral/political philosophy of discussions of race and white supremacy would lead one to think that race and racism have been marginal to the history of the West. And this belief is reinforced by the mainstream conceptualizations of the polity themselves, which portray it as essentially raceless, whether in the dominant view of an individualist liberal democracy or in the minority radical Marxist view of a class society. So it is not that mainstream contractarians have *no* picture. (Indeed it is impossible to theorize without *some* picture.) Rather, they have an *actual* (tacit) picture, which, in its exclusion or marginalization of race and its typically sanitized, whitewashed, and amnesiac account of European imperialism and settlement, is deeply flawed and misleading. So the powerful image of the idealized contract, in the absence of an explicit *counter*image, continues to shape our descriptive as well as normative theorizations. By providing *no* history, contemporary contractarianism encourages its audience to fill in a *mystified* history, which turns out to look oddly like the (ostensibly) repudiated history in the original contract itself! No one actually believes nowadays, of course, that people formally came out of the wilderness and signed a contract. But there *is* the impression that the modern European nation-states were not centrally affected by their imperial history and that societies such as the United States were founded on noble moral principles meant to include everyone, but unfortunately, there were some deviations.[73] *The "Racial Contract" explodes this picture as mythical, identifying it as itself an artifact of the Racial Contract in the second, de facto phase of white supremacy.* Thus—in the standard array of metaphors of perceptual/conceptual revolution—it effects a gestalt shift, reversing figure and ground, switching paradigms, inverting "norm" and "deviation," to emphasize that *nonwhite racial exclusion from personhood was the actual norm.* Racism, racial self-identification, and race thinking are then not in the least "surprising," "anomalous," "puzzling," incongruent with Enlightenment European humanism, but *required* by the Racial Contract as part of the terms for the European appropriation of the world. So in a sense standard contractarian discussions are fundamentally misleading, because they have things backward to begin with: what has usually been taken (when it has been noticed at all) as the racist "exception" has really been the *rule;* what has been taken as the "rule," the ideal norm, has really been the *exception.*

The second, related reason that the "Racial Contract" should be part of the necessary foundation for contemporary political theory is that our theorizing and moralizing *about* the sociopolitical facts are affected in characteristic ways by social structure. There is a reflexiveness to political theory, in which it theorizes about itself and later theorists critique the blindnesses of earlier ones. The classic texts of the central thinkers of the Western political tradition—for example, Plato, Hobbes, Locke, Burke, Marx—typically provide not merely normative judgments but mappings of social ontologies and political epistemologies which explain why the normative judgments of others have gone astray. These theorists recognized that to bring about the *ideal* polity, one needs to understand how the structure and workings of the *actual* polity may interfere with our perception of the social truth. Our characteristic patterns of understanding and misunderstanding of the world are themselves influenced by the way the world is and by the way we ourselves are, whether naturally or as shaped and molded by that world.

So one needs criteria for political knowing, whether through penetrating the illusory appearances of this empirical world (Plato), through learning to discern natural law (Hobbes, Locke), through rejecting abstraction for the accumulated wisdom of "prejudice" (Burke), or through demystifying oneself of bourgeois and patriarchal ideology (Marxism, feminism). Particularly for alternative, oppositional theory (as with the last two), the claim will be that an oppressive polity characterized by group domination distorts our cognizing in ways that themselves need to be theorized about. We are blinded to realities that we should see, taking for granted as natural what are in fact human-created structures. So we need to see differently, ridding ourselves of class and gender bias, coming to recognize as political what we had previously thought of as apolitical or personal, doing conceptual innovation, reconceiving the familiar, looking with new eyes at the old world around us.

Now if the "Racial Contract" is right, existing conceptions of the polity are foundationally deficient. There is obviously

123

all the difference in the world between saying the system is basically sound despite some unfortunate racist deviations, and saying that the polity is racially structured, the state white-supremacist, and races themselves significant existents that an adequate political ontology needs to accommodate. So the dispute would be not merely about the facts but about *why* these facts have gone so long unapprehended and untheorized in white moral/political theory. Could it be that membership in the *Herrenvolk*, the race privileged by this political system, tends to prevent recognition of it *as* a political system? Indeed, it could. So not only would meeting this political challenge imply a radically different "metanarrative" of the history that has brought us to this point, but it would also require, as I have sketched, a rethinking and reconceptualization of the existing conventional moral/political apparatus and a self-consciously reflexive epistemic examination of how this deficient apparatus has affected the moral psychology of whites and directed their attention away from certain realities. By its crucial silence on race and the corresponding opacities of its conventional conceptual array, the raceless social contract and the raceless world of contemporary moral and political theory render mysterious the actual political issues and concerns that have historically preoccupied a large section of the world's population.

Think of the rich colorful tapestry over the last two centuries of abolitionism, racial vindicationism, aboriginal land claims, antiimperial and anticolonial movements, antiapartheid struggle, searches to reclaim racial and cultural heritages, and ask yourself what thread of it ever appears within the bleached weave of the standard First World political philosophy text. It is undeniable (one would think) that these struggles are political, but dominant categories obscure our understanding of them. They seem to be taking place in a different conceptual space from the one inhabited by mainstream political theory. One will search in vain for them in most standard histories and contemporary surveys of Western political thought. The recent advent of discussions of "multiculturalism" is welcome, but what needs to be appreciated is that these are issues of political *power*, not just mutual misconceptions resulting from the clash of cultures. To the extent that "race" is assimilated to "ethnicity," white supremacy remains unmentioned, and the historic Racial Contract–prescribed connection between race and personhood is ignored, these discussions, in my opinion, fail to make the necessary drastic theoretical correction. Thus they still take place within a conventional, if expanded, framework. If I am right, what needs to be recognized is that side by side with the existing political structures familiar to all of us, the standard subject matter of political theory—absolutism and constitutionalism, dictatorship and democracy, capitalism and socialism—there has also been an unnamed global political structure—*global white supremacy*—and these struggles are in part struggles against this system. Until the system is named and seen as such, no serious theoretical appreciation of the significance of these phenomena is possible.

Another virtue of the "Racial Contract" is that it simultaneously recognizes the *reality* of race (causal power, theoretical centrality) and demystifies race (positing race as constructed).[74] Historically, the most influential theories of race have themselves been racist, varieties of more or less sophisticated biological determinism, from naive pre-Darwinian speculations to the later more elaborated views of nineteenth-century Social Darwinism and twentieth-century Nazi *Rassenkunde*, race science. To speak of "race theory" in the officially nonracist climate of today is thus likely to trigger alarm bells: hasn't it been proven that race is unreal? But it is a false dichotomization to assume that the only alternatives are race as nonexistent and race as biological essence. Contemporary "critical race theory"—of which this book could be seen as an example—adds the adjective specifically to differentiate itself from the essentialist views of the past.[75] *Race is sociopolitical rather than biological, but it is nonetheless real.*

Thus, on the one hand, unlike mainstream white theory, liberal *and* radical, the "Racial Contract" sees that "race" and "white supremacy" are themselves critical theoretical terms that must be incorporated into the vocabulary of an adequate sociopolitical theory, that society is neither just a collection of atomic individuals nor just a structure of workers and capitalists. On the other hand, the "Racial Contract" demystifies race, distancing itself from the "oppositional" biological determinisms (melanin theory, "sun people" and "ice people") and occasional deplorable anti-Semitism of some recent elements of the black tradition, as the 1960s promise of integration fails and intransigent social structures and growing white recalcitrance are increasingly conceptualized in naturalistic terms.

The "Racial Contract" thus places itself within the sensible mainstream of moral theory by not holding people responsible for what they cannot help. Even liberal whites of good will are sometimes made uneasy by racial politics, because an unsophisticatedly undifferentiated denunciatory vocabulary ("white") does not seem to allow for standard political/moral distinctions between a politics of choice—absolutist and democrat, fascist and liberal—for which it is rational that we should be held responsible, and a skin color and phenotype that, after all, we cannot help. By recognizing it as a political system, the "Racial Contract" *voluntarizes* race in the same way that the social contract voluntarizes the creation of society and the state. It distinguishes between whiteness as phenotype/genealogy and Whiteness as a political commitment to white supremacy, thus making conceptual room for "white renegades" and "race traitors." And its aim is not to replace one Racial Contract with another of a different color but ultimately to eliminate race (not as innocent human variety but as ontological superiority and inferiority, as differential entitlement and privilege) altogether.

Correspondingly, the "Racial Contract" demystifies the uniqueness of white racism (for those who, understandably, see Europeans as *intrinsically* White) by locating it as the contingent outcome of a particular set of circumstances. It is proper, given both the historical record and the denial of it until recently, that white racism and white Whiteness should be the polemical focus of critique. But it is important not to lose sight of the fact that other subordinate Racial Contracts exist which do not involve white/nonwhite relations. In a sense, the "Racial Contract" decolorizes Whiteness by detaching it from whiteness, thereby demonstrating that in a parallel universe it could have been Yellowness, Redness, Brownness, or Blackness. Or, alternatively phrased, we could have had a yellow, red, brown, or black Whiteness: *Whiteness is not really a color at all, but a set of power relations.*

That it is, is illustrated by the only serious twentieth-century challenger to European domination: Japan. As I have mentioned throughout, their unique history has put the Japanese in the peculiar position of being, at different times, or even simultaneously by different systems, nonwhite by the global White Racial Contract, white by the local (Nazi) Racial Contract, and a (White) yellow by their own Yellow Racial Contract. In Asia the Japanese have long considered themselves the superior race, oppressing the Ainu in their own country and proclaiming during the 1930s a Pan-Asiatic mission to "unite the yellow races" under their leadership against white Western domination. The ruthlessness displayed on both sides during the Pacific War, a "war without mercy," arose in part because on both sides it was a *race* war, a war between conflicting systems of racial superiority, competing claims to the real Whiteness, pink or yellow. The headline of one Hearst paper summed it up: "The war in the Pacific is the World War, the War of Oriental Races against Occidental Races for. the Domination of the World."[76] As written during the Japanese occupation of China, from the 1937 Rape of Nanking on, the Yellow Racial Contract produced a death toll estimated by some to be as high as 10–13 million people.[77]

What Axis triumph might have meant for the world is revealed in a remarkable document that survived the desperate burning of files in the last weeks before the arrival in Tokyo of the occupying U.S. army: *An Investigation of Global Policy with the Yamato Race as Nucleus*. Not exactly an equivalent to the infamous 1942 Nazi Wannsee Protocol that put the details of the Final Solution into place, it does nonetheless describe the "natural hierarchy based on inherent qualities and capabilities" of the various races of the world, envisages a global order in which the "Yamato race" would be the "leading race" (which would have to avoid intermarriage to maintain its purity), and prescribes a postwar mission of expansion and colonization based on an ominously revised global cartography in which, for example, America emerges as "Asia's eastern wing."[78] The Yamatos and the Aryans would, postvictory, have had to fight it out to decide who the real global master race was. So there is no reason to think that other nonwhites (nonyellows?) would have fared much better under this version of the Racial Contract. The point, then, is that while the White Racial Contract has historically been the most devastating and the most important one in shaping the contours of the world, it is not unique, and there should be no essentialist illusions about anyone's intrinsic "racial" virtue. All peoples can fall into Whiteness under the appropriate circumstances, as shown by the ("White") black Hutus' 1994 massacre of half a million to a million inferior black Tutsis in a few bloody weeks in Rwanda.

Though it may appear to be such, the "Racial Contract" is not a "deconstruction" of the social contract. I am in some sympathy with postmodernism politically—the iconoclastic challenge to orthodox theory, the tipping over of the white marble busts in the museum of Great Western Thinkers—but ultimately, I see it as an epistemological and theoretical dead end, itself symptomatic rather than diagnostic of the problems of the globe as we enter the new millennium.[79] The "Racial Contract" is really in the spirit of a racially informed *Ideologiekritik* and thus pro-Enlightenment (Jürgen Habermas's radical and to-be-completed Enlightenment, that is—though Habermas's Eurocentric, deraced, and deimperialized vision of modernity itself stands in need of critique)[80] and antipostmodernist. It criticizes the social contract from a normative base that does not see the ideals of contractarianism themselves as necessarily problematic but shows how they have been betrayed by white contractarians. So it assumes intertranslatability, the conceptual commensurability of degraded norm and critique, and brings them together in an epistemic union that repudiates the postmodernist picture of isolated, mutually unintelligible language games. Moreover, it is explicitly predicated on the *truth* of a particular metanarrative, the historical account of the European conquest of the world, which has made the world what it is today. Thus it lays claims to truth, objectivity, realism, the description of the world as it actually is, the prescription for a transformation of that world to achieve racial justice—and invites criticism on those same terms.

In the best tradition of oppositional materialist critique of hegemonic idealist social theory, the "Racial Contract" *recognizes the actuality of the world we live in*, relates the construction of ideals, and the *non*realization of these ideals, to the character of this world, to group interests and institutionalized structures, and points to what would be necessary for achieving them. Thus it unites description and prescription, fact and norm.

Unlike the social contract, which is necessarily embarrassed by the actual histories of the polities in which it is propagated, the "Racial Contract" *starts from* these uncomfortable realities. Thus it is not, like the social contract, continually forced to retreat into illusory idealizing abstraction, the never-never land of pure theory, but can move readily between the hypothetical and the actual, the subjunctive and the indicative, having no need to pretend things happened which did not, to evade and to elide and to skim over. The "Racial Contract" is intimate with the world and so is not continually "astonished" by revelations about it; it does not find it remarkable that racism has been the norm and that people think of themselves as raced rather than abstract citizens, which any objective history will in fact show. The "Racial Contract" is an abstraction that is *this*-worldly, showing that the problem with mainstream political philosophy is not abstraction in itself (all theory definitionally requires abstraction), but abstraction that, as Onora O'Neill has pointed out, characteristically abstracts away from the things that matter, the actual causal determinants and their requisite theoretical correlates, guided by the terms of the Racial Contract which has now written itself out of existence but continues to affect theory and theorizing by its invisible presence.[81] The "Racial Contract" throws open the doors of orthodox political philosophy's hermetically sealed, stuffy little universe and lets the world rush into its sterile white halls, a world populated not by abstract

citizens but by white, black, brown, yellow, red beings, inter-
acting with, pretending not to see, categorizing, judging, nego-
tiating, allying, exploiting, struggling with each other in large
measure according to race—the world, in short, in which we
all actually live.

Finally, the "Racial Contract" locates itself proudly in the
long, honorable tradition of oppositional black theory, the
theory of those who were denied the capacity to theorize, the
cognitions of persons rejecting their official subpersonhood.
The peculiar terms of the slavery contract meant that, of all
the different varieties of subpersons, blacks were the ones
most directly confronted over a period of hundreds of years
with the contradictions of white theory, being both a part
and not a part of the white polity, and as such epistemically
privileged. The "Racial Contract" pays tribute to the insights
of generations of anonymous "race men" (and "race women")
who, under the most difficult circumstances, often self-
educated, denied access to formal training and the resources
of the academy, the object of scorn and contempt from hegemonic white theory, nevertheless managed to forge the concepts necessary to trace the contours of the system oppressing
them, defying the massive weight of a white scholarship that
either morally justified this oppression or denied its existence.

Black activists have always recognized white domination,
white power (what one writer in 1919 called the "white-
ocracy," rule by whites),[82] as a political system of exclusion
and differential privilege, problematically conceptualized by
the categories of either white liberalism or white Marxism.
The "Racial Contract" can thus be regarded as a black vernacular (literally: "the language of the slave") "Signifyin(g)" on
the social contract, a "double-voiced," "two-toned," "formal
revision" that "critique[s] the nature of (white) meaning itself," by demonstrating that "a simultaneous, but negated,

parallel discursive (ontological, political) universe exists within the larger white discursive universe."[83] It is a black demystification of the lies of white theory, an uncovering of the Klan robes beneath the white politician's three-piece suit. Ironic, cool, hip, above all *knowing*, the "Racial Contract" speaks from the perspective of the cognizers whose mere presence in the halls of white theory is a cognitive threat, because—in the inverted epistemic logic of the racial polity—the "ideal speech situation" requires our absence, since we are, literally, the men and women *who know too much*, who—in that wonderful American expression—*know where the bodies are buried* (after all, so many of them are our own). It does what black critique has always had to do to be effective: it situates itself in the same space as its adversary and then shows what follows from "writing 'race' and [seeing] the difference it makes."[84] As such, it makes it possible for us to connect the two rather than, as at present, have them isolated in two ghettoized spaces, black political theory's ghettoization from mainstream discussion, white mainstream theory's ghettoization from reality.

The struggle to close the gap between the ideal of the social contract and the reality of the Racial Contract has been the unacknowledged political history of the past few hundred years, the "battle of the color line," in the words of W. E. B. Du Bois, and is likely to continue being so for the near future, as racial division continues to fester, the United States moves demographically from a white-majority to a nonwhite-majority society, the chasm between a largely white First World and a largely nonwhite Third World continues to deepen, desperate illegal immigration from the latter to the former escalates, and demands for global justice in a new world order of "global apartheid" grow louder.[85] Naming this reality brings it into the necessary theoretical focus for these issues to be honestly addressed. Those who pretend not to see them, who claim not to recognize the picture I have sketched, are only continuing the epistemology of ignorance required by the original Racial Contract. As long as this studied ignorance persists, the Racial Contract will only be rewritten, rather than being torn up altogether, and justice will continue to be restricted to "just us."

NOTES

INTRODUCTION

1. A 1994 report on American philosophy, "Status and Future of
   the Profession," revealed that "only one department in 20 (28
   of the 456 departments reporting) has any [tenure-track] African-
   American faculty, with slightly fewer having either Hispanic-
   American or Asian-American [tenure-track] faculty (17 departments in both cases). A mere seven departments have any
   [tenure-track] Native American faculty." *Proceedings and Addresses of The American Philosophical Association* 70, no. 2
   (1996): 137.
2. For an overview, see, for example, Ernest Barker, Introduction
   to *Social Contract: Essays by Locke, Hume, and Rousseau*, ed.
   Barker (1947; rpt. Oxford: Oxford University Press, 1960); Michael Lessnoff, *Social Contract* (Atlantic Highlands, N.J.: Humanities Press, 1986); Will Kymlicka, "The Social Contract
   Tradition," in *A Companion to Ethics*, ed. Peter Singer (Oxford:
   Blackwell Reference, 1991), pp. 186–96; Jean Hampton, "Contract and Consent," in *A Companion to Contemporary Political
   Philosophy*, ed. Robert E. Goodin and Philip Pettit (Oxford:
   Blackwell Reference, 1993), pp. 379–93.
3. Indigenous peoples as a global group are sometimes referred to
   as the "Fourth World." See Roger Moody, ed., *The Indigenous
   Voice: Visions and Realities*, 2d ed., rev. (1988; rpt. Utrecht:
   International Books, 1993).

4. For a praiseworthy exception, see Iris Marion Young, *Justice and the Politics of Difference* (Princeton: Princeton University Press, 1990). Young focuses explicitly on the implications for standard conceptions of justice of group subordination, including racial groups.

5. Credit for the revival of social contract theory, and indeed postwar political philosophy in general, is usually given to John Rawls, *A Theory of Justice* (Cambridge: Harvard University Press, 1971).

6. Thomas Hobbes, *Leviathan*, ed. Richard Tuck (Cambridge: Cambridge University Press, 1991); John Locke, *Two Treatises of Government*, ed. Peter Laslett (1960; rpt. Cambridge: Cambridge University Press, 1988); Jean-Jacques Rousseau, *Discourse on the Origins and Foundations of Inequality among Men*, trans. Maurice Cranston (London: Penguin, 1984); Rousseau, *The Social Contract*, trans. Maurice Cranston (London: Penguin, 1968); Immanuel Kant, *The Metaphysics of Morals*, trans. Mary Gregor (Cambridge: Cambridge University Press, 1991).

7. In "Contract and Consent," p. 382, Jean Hampton reminds us that for the classic theorists, contract is intended "simultaneously to describe the nature of political societies, and to prescribe a new and more defensible form for such societies." In this essay, and also in "The Contractarian Explanation of the State," in *The Philosophy of the Human Sciences*, Midwest Studies in Philosophy, 15, ed. Peter A. French, Theodore E. Uehling Jr., and Howard K. Wettstein (Notre Dame, Ind.: University of Notre Dame Press, 1990), pp. 344–71, she argues explicitly for a revival of the old-fashioned, seemingly discredited "contractarian explanation of the state." Hampton points out that the imagery of "contract" captures the essential point that "authoritative political societies are human creations" (not divinely ordained or naturally determined) and *"conventionally* generated."

8. Rousseau, *Discourse on Inequality*, pt. 2.

9. Carole Pateman, *The Sexual Contract* (Stanford: Stanford University Press, 1988). One difference between our approaches is that Pateman thinks contractarianism is *necessarily* oppressive—"Contract always generates political right in the form of relations of domination and subordination" (p. 8)—

whereas I see domination within contract theory as more contingent. For me, in other words, it is not the case that a Racial Contract *had* to underpin the social contract. Rather, this contract is a result of the particular conjunction of circumstances in global history which led to European imperialism. And as a corollary, I believe contract theory can be put to positive use once this hidden history is acknowledged, though I do not follow up such a program in this book. For an example of feminist contractarianism that contrasts with Pateman's negative assessment, see Susan Moller Okin, *Justice, Gender, and the Family* (New York: Basic Books, 1989).

10. See, for example, Paul Thagard, *Conceptual Revolutions* (Princeton: Princeton University Press, 1992), p. 22.

11. See Hampton, "Contract and Consent" and "Contractarian Explanation." Hampton's own focus is the liberal-democratic state, but obviously her strategy of employing "contract" to conceptualize conventionally generated norms and practices is open to be adapted to the understanding of the *non*-liberal-democratic *racial* state, the difference being that "the people" now become the white population.

CHAPTER 1. OVERVIEW

1. Otto Gierke termed these respectively the *Gesellschaftsvertrag* and the *Herrschaftsvertrag*. For a discussion, see, for example, Barker, Introduction, *Social Contract*; and Lessnoff, *Social Contract*, chap. 3.

2. Rawls, *Theory of Justice*, pt. 1.

3. In speaking generally of "whites," I am not, of course, denying that there are gender relations of domination and subordination or, for that matter, class relations of domination and subordination within the white population. I am not claiming that race is the only axis of social oppression. But race is what I want to focus on; so in the absence of that chimerical entity, a unifying theory of race, class, and gender oppression, it seems to me that one has to make generalizations that it would be stylistically cumbersome to qualify at every point. So these should just be

taken as read. Nevertheless, I do want to insist that my overall picture is roughly accurate, i.e., that whites *do* in general benefit from white supremacy (though gender and class differentiation mean, of course, that they do not benefit equally) and that historically white racial solidarity *has* overridden class and gender solidarity. Women, subordinate classes, and nonwhites may be oppressed in common, but it is not a common oppression: the structuring is so different that it has not led to any common front between them. Neither white women nor white workers have *as a group* (as against principled individuals) historically made common cause with nonwhites against colonialism, white settlement, slavery, imperialism, jim crow, apartheid. We all have multiple identities, and, to this extent, most of us are both privileged and disadvantaged by different systems of domination. But white racial identity has generally triumphed over all others; it *is* race that (transgender, transclass) has generally determined the social world and loyalties, the lifeworld, of whites—whether as citizens of the colonizing mother country, settlers, nonslaves, or beneficiaries of the "color bar" and the "color line." There has been no comparable, spontaneously crystallizing transracial "workers'" world or transracial "female" world: race is the identity around which whites have usually closed ranks. Nevertheless, as a concession, a semantic signal of this admitted gender privileging within the white population, by which white women's personhood is originally virtual, dependent on their having the appropriate relation (daughter, sister, wife) to the white male, I will sometimes deliberately use the non-gender-neutral "men." For some recent literature on these problematic intersections of identity, see, for example, Ruth Frankenberg, *White Women, Race Matters: The Social Construction of Whiteness* (Minneapolis: University of Minnesota Press, 1993); Nupur Chaudhuri and Margaret Strobel, eds., *Western Women and Imperialism: Complicity and Resistance* (Bloomington: Indiana University Press, 1992); David Roediger, *The Wages of Whiteness: Race and the Making of the American Working Class* (London: Verso, 1991).

4. Rousseau, *Social Contract*; Hobbes, *Leviathan*.
5. For a discussion of the two versions, see Kymlicka, "The Social Contract Tradition."

6. Hobbes's judgment that "INJUSTICE, is no other than *the not Performance of Covenant," Leviathan*, p. 100, has standardly been taken as a statement of moral conventionalism. Hobbes's egalitarian social morality is based not on the moral equality of humans, but on the fact of a rough parity of physical power and mental ability in the state of nature (chap. 13). Within this framework, the Racial Contract would then be the natural outcome of a systematic *disparity* in power—of weaponry rather than individual strength—between expansionist Europe and the rest of the world. This could be said to be neatly summed up in Hilaire Belloc's famous little ditty: "Whatever happens, we have got/The Maxim Gun, and they have not." Hilaire Belloc, "The Modern Traveller," quoted in John Ellis, *The Social History of the Machine Gun* (1975; rpt. Baltimore: Johns Hopkins Paperbacks, 1986), p. 94. Or at an earlier stage, in the conquest of the Americas, the musket and the steel sword.

7. See, for example, A. P. d'Entrèves, *Natural Law: An Introduction to Legal Philosophy*, 2d rev. ed. (1951; rpt. London: Hutchinson, 1970).

8. Locke, *Second Treatise* of *Two Treatises of Government*, p. 269.

9. Kant, *Metaphysics of Morals*, pp. 230–32.

10. See Arthur O. Lovejoy, *The Great Chain of Being: A Study of the History of an Idea* (Cambridge: Harvard University Press, 1948).

11. For the notion of "epistemological communities," see recent work in feminist theory—for example, Linda Alcoff and Elizabeth Potter, eds., *Feminist Epistemologies* (New York: Routledge, 1993).

12. Thus Ward Churchill, a Native American, speaks sardonically of "fantasies of the master race." Ward Churchill, *Fantasies of the Master Race: Literature, Cinema, and the Colonization of American Indians*, ed. M. Annette Jaimes (Monroe, Maine: Common Courage Press, 1992); William Gibson, *Neuromancer* (New York: Ace Science Fiction Books, 1984).

13. Robert Young, *White Mythologies: Writing History and the West* (London: Routledge, 1990); Edward W. Said, *Orientalism* (1978; rpt. New York: Vintage Books, 1979); V. Y. Mudimbe, *The Invention of Africa: Gnosis, Philosophy, and the Order of Knowledge* (Bloomington: Indiana University Press, 1988); Enrique Dussel,

The Invention of the Americas: Eclipse of "the Other" and the Myth of Modernity, trans. Michael D. Barber (1992; rpt. New York: Continuum, 1995); Robert Berkhofer Jr., *The White Man's Indian: Images of the American Indian from Columbus to the Present* (New York: Knopf, 1978); Gretchen M. Bataille and Charles L. P. Silet, eds., *The Pretend Indians: Images of Native Americans in the Movies* (Ames: Iowa State University Press, 1980); George M. Fredrickson, *The Black Image in the White Mind: The Debate on Afro-American Character and Destiny, 1817–1914* (1971; rpt. Hanover, N.H.: Wesleyan University Press, 1987); Roberto Fernández Retamar, *Caliban and Other Essays*, trans. Edward Baker (Minneapolis: University of Minnesota Press, 1989); Peter Hulme, *Colonial Encounters: Europe and the Native Caribbean, 1492–1797* (1986; rpt. London: Routledge, 1992).

14. Frederick Engels, *The Origin of the Family, Private Property, and the State* (New York: International, 1972), p. 120.

15. Jean-Paul Sartre, Preface to Frantz Fanon, *The Wretched of the Earth*, trans. Constance Farrington (1961; rpt. New York: Grove Weidenfeld, 1991).

16. V. G. Kiernan, *The Lords of Human Kind: Black Man, Yellow Man, and White Man in an Age of Empire* (1969; rpt. New York: Columbia University Press, 1986); Anthony Pagden, *Lords of All the World: Ideologies of Empire in Spain, Britain, and France, c. 1500–c. 1800* (New Haven: Yale University Press, 1995).

17. Pagden, *Lords*, pp. 1–2.

18. Robert A. Williams Jr., "The Algebra of Federal Indian Law: The Hard Trail of Decolonizing and Americanizing the White Man's Indian Jurisprudence," *Wisconsin Law Review* 1986 (1986): 229. See also Robert A. Williams Jr., *The American Indian in Western Legal Thought: The Discourses of Conquest* (New York: Oxford University Press, 1990).

19. Williams, "Algebra," pp. 230–31, 233. See also Lewis Hanke, *Aristotle and the American Indians: A Study in Race Prejudice in the Modern World* (Bloomington: Indiana University Press, 1959), p. 19.

20. Williams, "Algebra"; Hanke, *Aristotle*.

21. Allen Carey-Webb, "Other-Fashioning: The Discourse of Empire

and Nation in Lope de Vega's *El Nuevo mundo descubierto por Cristobal Colon*," in *Amerindian Images and the Legacy of Columbus*, ed. René Jara and Nicholas Spadaccini, Hispanic Issues, 9 (Minneapolis: University of Minnesota Press, 1992), pp. 433-34.

22. Philip D. Curtin, Introduction, to *Imperialism*, ed. Curtin (New York: Walker, 1971), p. xiii.

23. Pierre L. van den Berghe, *Race and Racism: A Comparative Perspective*, 2d ed. (New York: Wiley, 1978).

24. Pagden, *Lords*, chap. 1.

25. Williams, "Algebra," p. 253.

26. Justice Joseph Story, quoted in Williams, "Algebra," p. 256.

27. *Dred Scott v. Sanford*, 1857, in *Race, Class, and Gender in the United States: An Integrated Study*, ed. Paula S. Rothenberg, 3d ed. (New York: St. Martin's Press, 1995), p. 323.

28. Excerpt from Jules Harmand, *Domination et colonisation* (1910), in Curtin, *Imperialism*, pp. 294-98.

29. Edward W. Said, *Culture and Imperialism* (New York: Knopf, 1993), pp. xiv, xiii.

30. Harold R. Isaacs, "Color in World Affairs," *Foreign Affairs* 47 (1969): 235, 246. See also Benjamin P. Bowser, ed., *Racism and Anti-Racism in World Perspective* (Thousand Oaks, Calif: Sage, 1995).

31. Helen Jackson, *A Century of Dishonor: A Sketch of the United States Government's Dealings with Some of the Indian Tribes* (1881; rpt. New York: Indian Head Books, 1993). In her classic exposé, Jackson concludes (pp. 337-38): "It makes little difference . . . where one opens the record of the history of the Indians; every page and every year has its dark stain. The story of one tribe is the story of all, varied only by differences of time and place. . . . [T]he United States Government breaks promises now [1880] as deftly as then [1795], and with an added ingenuity from long practice." Jackson herself, it should be noted, saw Native Americans as having a "lesser right," since there was no question about the "fairness of holding that ultimate sovereignty belonged to the civilized discoverer, as against the savage barbarian." To think otherwise would merely be "feeble sentimentalism" (pp. 10-11). But she did at least want this lesser right recognized.

32. See, for example, David E. Stannard, *American Holocaust: Columbus and the Conquest of the New World* (New York: Oxford University Press, 1992).

33. Richard Drinnon, *Facing West: The Metaphysics of Indian-Hating and Empire-Building* (New York: Meridian, 1980), p. 332.

34. Ibid., p. 102. See also Reginald Horsman, *Race and Manifest Destiny: The Origins of American Racial Anglo-Saxonism* (Cambridge: Harvard University Press, 1981); and Ronald Takaki, *Iron Cages: Race and Culture in 19th-Century America* (1979; rpt. New York: Oxford University Press, 1990).

35. A. Grenfell Price, *White Settlers and Native Peoples: An Historical Study of Racial Contacts between English-Speaking Whites and Aboriginal Peoples in the United States, Canada, Australia, and New Zealand* (1950; rpt. Westport, Conn.: Greenwood Press, 1972); A. Grenfell Price, *The Western Invasions of the Pacific and Its Continents* (Oxford: Clarendon Press, 1963); van den Berghe, *Race*; Louis Hartz, *The Founding of New Societies: Studies in the History of the United States, Latin America, South Africa, Canada, and Australia* (New York: Harcourt, Brace, and World, 1964); F. S. Stevens, ed., *Racism: The Australian Experience*, 3 vols. (New York: Taplinger, 1972); Henry Reynolds, *The Other Side of the Frontier: Aboriginal Resistance to the European Invasion of Australia* (Harmondsworth, Middlesex: Penguin, 1982). Price's books are valuable sources in comparative history, but—though progressive by the standards of the time—they need to be treated with caution, since their figures and attitudes are both now somewhat dated. In *White Settlers*, for example, the Indian population north of the Rio Grande is estimated at fewer than 850,000, whereas estimates today are ten to twenty times higher, and Price speculates that the Indians were "less advanced than their white conquerors" because they had smaller brains (pp. 6–7).

36. Van den Berghe, *Race*, p. 18.

37. C. Vann Woodward, *The Strange Career of Jim Crow*, 3d ed. (1955; rpt. New York: Oxford University Press, 1974); George M. Fredrickson, *White Supremacy: A Comparative Study in American and South African History* (New York: Oxford University Press, 1981); Douglas S. Massey and Nancy A. Denton,

American Apartheid: Segregation and the Making of the Under-class (Cambridge: Harvard University Press, 1993).

38. See, for example, Kiernan, *Lords;* V. G. Kiernan, *Imperialism and its Contradictions,* ed. Harvey J. Kaye (New York: Routledge, 1995); D. K. Fieldhouse, *The Colonial Empires: A Comparative Survey from the Eighteenth Century* (1966; rpt. London: Macmillan, 1982); Pagden, *Lords;* Chinweizu, *The West and the Rest of Us: White Predators, Black Slavers, and the African Elite* (New York: Vintage Books, 1975); Henri Brunschwig, *French Colonialism, 1871–1914: Myths and Realities,* trans. William Granville Brown (1964.; rpt. New York: Praeger, 1966); David Healy, *U.S. Expansionism: The Imperialist Urge in the 1890s* (Madison: University of Wisconsin Press, 1970).

39. Said, *Culture,* p. 8.

40. Kiernan, *Lords,* p. 24.

41. Linda Alcoff outlines an attractive, distinctively Latin American ideal of hybrid racial identity in her "Mestizo Identity," in *American Mixed Race: The Culture of Microdiversity,* ed. Naomi Zack (Lanham, Md.: Rowman and Littlefield, 1995), pp. 257–78. Unfortunately, however, this ideal has yet to be realized. For an exposure of the Latin American myths of "racial democracy" and a race-transcendent *mestizaje,* and an account of the reality of the ideal of *blanqueamiento* (whitening) and the continuing subordination of blacks and the darker-skinned throughout the region, see, for example, Minority Rights Group, ed., *No Longer Invisible: Afro-Latin Americans Today* (London: Minority Rights, 1995); and Bowser, *Racism and Anti-Racism.*

42. Locke, *Second Treatise,* pp. 350–51. Since Locke also uses "property" to mean rights, this is not quite as one-dimensional a vision of government as it sounds.

43. Hobbes, *Leviathan,* p. 89.

44. W. E. B. Du Bois, *Black Reconstruction in America, 1860–1880* (1935; rpt. New York: Atheneum, 1992).

45. See Eric Jones, *The European Miracle* (Cambridge: Cambridge University Press, 1981). My discussion here follows J. M. Blaut et al., *1492: The Debate on Colonialism, Eurocentrism, and History* (Trenton, N.J.: Africa World Press, 1992); and J. M. Blaut,

The Colonizer's Model of the World: Geographical Diffusionism and Eurocentric History (New York: Guilford Press, 1993).

46. Blaut, *1492*; Blaut, *Colonizer's Model*.

47. Sandra Harding, Introduction, to Harding, ed., *The "Racial" Economy of Science: Toward a Democratic Future* (Bloomington: Indiana University Press, 1993), p. 2.

48. Eric Williams, *Capitalism and Slavery* (1944; rpt. New York: Capricorn Books, 1966).

49. Walter Rodney, *How Europe Underdeveloped Africa* (1972; rpt. Washington, D.C.: Howard University Press, 1974); Samir Amin, *Eurocentrism*, trans. Russell Moore (1988: rpt. New York: Monthly Review Press, 1989); André Gunder Frank, *World Accumulation, 1492–1789* (New York: Monthly Review Press, 1978); Immanuel Wallerstein, *The Modern World System*, 3 vols. (New York: Academic Press, 1974–1988).

50. Blaut, *1492*, p. 3.

51. Kiernan, *Imperialism*, pp. 98, 149.

52. Quoted in Noam Chomsky, *Year 501: The Conquest Continues* (Boston: South End Press, 1993), p. 61.

53. But see Richard J. Herrnstein and Charles Murray's bestseller *The Bell Curve: Intelligence and Class Structure in American Life* (New York: Free Press, 1994), as a sign that the older, straightforwardly racist theories may be making a comeback.

54. See, for example: Andrew Hacker, *Two Nations: Black and White, Separate, Hostile, Unequal* (New York: Scribner's, 1992); Derrick Bell, *Faces at the Bottom of the Well: The Permanence of Racism* (New York: BasicBooks, 1992); Massey and Denton, *American Apartheid*; Stephen Steinberg, *Turning Back: The Retreat from Racial Justice in American Thought and Policy* (Boston: Beacon Press, 1995); Donald R. Kinder and Lynn M. Sanders, *Divided by Color: Racial Politics and Democratic Ideals* (Chicago: University of Chicago Press, 1996); Tom Wicker, *Tragic Failure: Racial Integration in America* (New York: William Morrow, 1996).

55. Melvin L. Oliver and Thomas M. Shapiro, *Black Wealth/White Wealth: A New Perspective on Racial Inequality* (New York: Routledge 1995), pp. 86, 7.

56. Richard F. America, ed., *The Wealth of Races: The Present Value*

of Benefits from Past Injustices (New York: Greenwood Press, 1990). For another ironic tribute, whose subject is the international distribution of wealth, see Malcolm Caldwell, *The Wealth of Some Nations* (London: Zed Press, 1977).

57. David H. Swinton, "Racial Inequality and Reparations," in America, *Wealth of Races*, p. 156.

58. James Marketti, "Estimated Present Value of Income Diverted during Slavery," in America, *Wealth of Races*, p. 107.

59. Robert S. Browne, "Achieving Parity through Reparations," in America, *Wealth of Races*, p. 204; Swinton, "Racial Inequality," p. 156.

CHAPTER 2. DETAILS

1. I will later discuss the taxonomic problems posed by "borderline"/"semi-" Europeans.

2. See, for example, Jan Nederveen Pieterse, *White on Black: Images of Africa and Blacks in Western Popular Culture* (1990; rpt. New Haven: Yale University Press, 1992), pp. 30–31; Ronald Sanders, *Lost Tribes and Promised Lands: The Origins of American Racism* (Boston: Little, Brown, 1978), p. 202.

3. Edward Dudley and Maximillian E. Novak, eds., *The Wild Man Within: An Image in Western Thought from the Renaissance to Romanticism* (Pittsburgh: University of Pittsburgh Press, 1972).

4. Hayden White, "The Forms of Wildness: Archaeology of an Idea," in Dudley and Novak, *Wild Man*, p. 5.

5. Roy Harvey Pearce, *Savagism and Civilization: A Study of the Indian and the American Mind*, rev. ed. (1953; rpt. Baltimore: Johns Hopkins Press, 1965) (original title: *The Savages of America*), p. 3.

6. Mary Louise Pratt, "Humboldt and the Reinvention of America," in Jara and Spadaccini, *Amerindian Images*, p. 589.

7. Mudimbe, *Invention of Africa*, pp. 15, 13.

8. Martin Bernal, *The Fabrication of Ancient Greece, 1785–1985*, vol. 1 of *Black Athena: The Afroasiatic Roots of Classical Civilization* (New Brunswick, N.J.: Rutgers University Press, 1987), This claim has a long history in the international black commu-

nity (African, African American). See, for example, Cheikh Anta Diop, *The African Origin of Civilization: Myth or Reality*, trans. Mercer Cook (1955, 1967; rpt. Westport, Conn.: Lawrence Hill, 1974).

9. Harding, *"Racial" Economy*, p. 27.

10. Joseph Conrad, *Heart of Darkness*, ed. Paul O'Prey (1902; rpt. London: Penguin Books, 1983), p. 33.

11. Scott B. Cook, *Colonial Encounters in the Age of High Imperialism* (New York: HarperCollins World History Series, 1996), p. 104.

12. Mudimbe, *Invention of Africa*, p. 71.

13. Sanders, *Lost Tribes*, pp. 9–12.

14. Drinnon, *Facing West*, pp. 122–23, 105, 66.

15. For an analysis of the film, see, for example, Michael Ryan and Douglas Kellner, *Camera Politica: The Politics and Ideology of Contemporary Hollywood Film* (Bloomington: Indiana University Press, 1988).

16. David Theo Goldberg, *Racist Culture: Philosophy and the Politics of Meaning* (Cambridge, Mass.: Blackwell, 1993), p. 185, and more generally, chap. 8, "'Polluting the Body Politic': Race and Urban Location," pp. 185–205.

17. Fanon, *Wretched of the Earth*, pp. 38–40.

18. Franke Wilmer, *The Indigenous Voice in World Politics: Since Time Immemorial* (Newbury Park, Calif.: Sage, 1993).

19. Locke, *Second Treatise*, p. 301.

20. Francis Jennings, *The Invasion of America: Indians, Colonialism, and the Cant of Conquest* (1975; rpt. New York: Norton, 1976), pt. 1.

21. Ibid, p. 16. See also Stannard, *American Holocaust*, chaps. 1 and 2, for an account of the exponential upward revision in recent years of estimates of the pre-Columbian population of the Americas and the politics of its previous undercounting. Half a century ago, standard figures were 8 million total for North and South America and fewer than 1 million for the region north of Mexico; today some estimates would put these numbers as high as 145 million and 18 million, respectively. Stannard, *American Holocaust*, p. 11.

22. Drinnon, *Facing West*, pp. 49, 212, 232.

23. Quoted from an official document by A. Barrie Pittock, "Aboriginal Land Rights," in Stevens, *Racism* 2:192.

24. Leonard Thompson, *The Political Mythology of Apartheid* (New Haven: Yale University Press, 1985), p. 75.

25. Drinnon, *Facing West*, p. 213.

26. Russel Ward, "An Australian Legend," *Royal Australian Historical Society Journal and Proceedings* 47, no. 6 (1961): 344, quoted by M. C. Hartwig, "Aborigines and Racism: An Historical Perspective," in Stevens, *Racism* 2:9.

27. For a classic analysis, see Frantz Fanon, *Black Skin, White Masks*, trans. Charles Lam Markmann (1952; rpt. New York: Grove Weidenfeld, 1968); and for a recent exploration, Lewis R. Gordon, *Bad Faith and Antiblack Racism* (Atlantic Highlands, N.J.: Humanities Press, 1995), esp. chaps. 7, 14, and 15, pp. 29–44. 97–103, 104–16.

28. Gordon, *Bad Faith*, pp. 99, 105.

29. Frankenberg, *White Women*, chap. 3.

30. Fanon, *Black Skin*; Charles Herbert Stember, *Sexual Racism: The Emotional Barrier to an Integrated Society* (New York: Elsevier, 1976); John D'Emilio and Estelle B. Freedman, *Intimate Matters: A History of Sexuality in America* (New York: Harper and Row, 1988), chap. 5, "Race and Sexuality," pp. 85–108.

31. Susan Mendus, "Kant: 'An Honest but Narrow-Minded Bourgeois'?" in *Women in Western Political Philosophy*, ed. Ellen Kennedy and Susan Mendus (New York: St. Martin's Press, 1987), pp. 21–43.

32. Aristotle, *The Politics*, trans. T. A. Sinclair (1962; rev. ed. Harmondsworth, Middlesex: Penguin, 1981), pp. 63–73.

33. White, "Forms of Wildness," p. 17.

34. Jennings, *Invasion of America*, p. 6.

35. See Cornel West's description of the emergence in the modern period of the "normative gaze" of white supremacy: "A Genealogy of Modern Racism," chap. 2 of *Prophesy Deliverance!: An Afro-American Revolutionary Christianity* (Phildelphia: Westminster Press, 1982), pp. 47–65.

36. M.I. Finley, *Ancient Slavery and Modern Ideology* (New York: Viking Press, 1980), p. 144.

37. Lucius Outlaw Jr., "Life-Worlds, Modernity, and Philosophical

Praxis: Race, Ethnicity, and Critical Social Theory," in Outlaw, *On Race and Philosophy* (New York: Routledge, 1996), p. 165.

38. Quoted in Drinnon, *Facing West*, p. 75.

39. Said, *Culture and Imperialism*, pp. 52, 59.

40. Orlando Patterson, *Freedom in the Making of Western Culture*, vol. 1 of *Freedom* (New York: Basic Books, 1991).

41. Toni Morrison, *Playing in the Dark: Whiteness and the Literary Imagination* (Cambridge: Harvard University Press, 1992).

42. Quoted in Pearce, *Savagism*, pp. 7–8.

43. For a discussion, see, for example, Stephen Jay Gould, *The Mismeasure of Man* (New York and London: Norton, 1981); and William H. Tucker, *The Science and Politics of Racial Research* (Urbana: University of Illinois Press, 1994). Tucker asserts flatly (p. 5): "The truth is that though waged with scientific weapons, the goal in this controversy has always been political."

44. Harmannus Hoetink, *Caribbean Race Relations: A Study of Two Variants*, trans. Eva M. Hooykaas (1962; rpt. London: Oxford University Press, 1967).

45. George L. Mosse, *Toward the Final Solution: A History of European Racism* (1978; rpt. Madison: University of Wisconsin Press, 1985), pp. xii, 11.

46. Winthrop D. Jordan, *White over Black: American Attitudes toward the Negro, 1550–1812* (1968; rpt. New York: Norton, 1977).

47. Franklin, *Observations Concerning the Increase of Mankind* (1751), quoted in Jordan, *White over Black*, pp. 270, 143.

48. See, for example, Kathy Russell, Midge Wilson, and Ronald Hall, *The Color Complex: The Politics of Skin Color among African Americans* (New York: Harcourt Brace Jovanovich, 1992).

49. Frank M. Snowden Jr., *Blacks in Antiquity: Ethiopians in the Greco-Roman Experience* (Cambridge: Harvard University Press, 1970); Frank M. Snowden Jr., *Before Color Prejudice: The Ancient View of Blacks* (Cambridge: Harvard University Press, 1983).

50. Theodore W. Allen, *Racial Oppression and Social Control*, vol. 1 of *The Invention of the White Race* (New York: Verso, 1994); Ian F. Haney Lopez, *White by Law: The Legal Construction of Race* (New York: New York University Press, 1996).

51. Jennings, *Invasion of America*, p. 60.

52. Hugo Grotius, *The Law of War and Peace*, trans. Francis W. Kelsey (Indianapolis: Bobbs-Merrill, 1925), chap. 20, "On Punishments," of bk. 2, p. 506, quoted in Williams, "Algebra," p. 250.

53. For the following, compare James Tully, *Strange Multiplicity: Constitutionalism in an Age of Diversity* (Cambridge: Cambridge University Press, 1995), esp. chap. 3, "The Historical Formation of Modern Constitutionalism: The Empire of Uniformity," pp. 58–98. I thank Anthony Laden for bringing this book to my attention, which I only learned about when my own manuscript was on the verge of completion.

54. Hobbes, *Leviathan*, p. 89.

55. Richard Ashcraft, "Leviathan Triumphant: Thomas Hobbes and the Politics of Wild Men," in Dudley and Novak, *Wild Man*, pp. 146–47.

56. Hobbes, *Leviathan*, pp. 89–90.

57. Two hundred years later, by contrast, the British colonial enterprise, with the accompanying ontological dichotomization, was so well entrenched that John Stuart Mill experienced not the slightest qualm in asserting (in an essay now seen as a classic humanist defense of individualism and freedom) that the liberal harm principle "is meant to apply only to human beings in the maturity of their faculties," not to those "backward states of society in which the race itself may be considered as in its nonage": "Despotism is a legitimate mode of government in dealing with barbarians, provided the end be their improvement." John Stuart Mill, *On Liberty and Other Writings*, ed. Stefan Collini (Cambridge: Cambridge University Press, 1989), p. 13.

58. Locke, *Second Treatise*, chap. 5, "Of Property."

59. Robert A. Williams Jr., "Documents of Barbarism: The Contemporary Legacy of European Racism and Colonialism in the Narrative Traditions of Federal Indian Law," *Arizona Law Review* 237 (1989), excerpted in *Critical Race Theory: The Cutting Edge*, ed. Richard Delgado (Philadelphia: Temple University Press, 1995), p. 103.

60. Locke, *Second Treatise*, chap. 16, "On Conquest."

61. See, for example, Jennifer Welchman, "Locke on Slavery and

Inalienable Rights," *Canadian Journal of Philosophy* 25 (1995) 67–81.

62. Rousseau, *Discourse on Inequality*, pp. 83, 87, 90, 1 36, 140, 145 (nonwhite savages), 140 (European savages).

63. Ibid., p. 116.

64. Rousseau, *Social Contract*, bk. 1, chap. 8.

65. Emmanuel Eze, "The Color of Reason: The Idea of 'Race' in Kant's Anthropology," in *Anthropology and the German Enlightenment*, ed. Katherine Faull (Lewisburg, Pa.: Bucknell University Press, 1995), pp. 196–237.

66. Eze cites the 1950 judgment of Earl Count that scholars often forget that "Immanuel Kant produced the most profound raciological thought of the eighteenth century." Earl W. Count, ed., *This Is Race: An Anthology Selected from the International Literature on the Races of Man* (New York: Henry Schuman, 1950), p. 704, quoted in Eze, "Color of Reason," p. 196. Compare the 1967 verdict of the German anthropologist Wilhelm Mühlmann that Kant is "the founder of the modern concept of race," quoted in Leon Poliakov, "Racism from the Enlightenment to the Age of Imperialism," in *Racism and Colonialism*, ed. Robert Ross (The Hague: Leiden University Press, 1982), p. 59.

67. Mosse, *Final Solution*, pp. 30–31.

68. Immanuel Kant, *Observations on the Feeling of the Beautiful and Sublime*, trans. John T. Goldthwait (Berkeley: University of California Press, 1960), pp. 111–13.

69. Eze, "Color of Reason," pp. 214–15, 209–15, 217.

70. See David Lehman, *Signs of the Times: Deconstruction and the Fall of Paul de Man* (New York: Poseidon Press, 1991).

71. Janet L. Abu-Lughod, *Before European Hegemony: The World System, A.D. 1250–1350* (New York: Oxford University Press, 1989).

72. Fredric Jameson, "Modernism and Imperialism," in *Nationalism, Colonialism, and Literature*, ed. Seamus Deane (Minneapolis: University of Minnesota Press, 1990), pp. 50–51.

73. Steinberg, *Turning Back*, p. 152.

74. Massey and Denton, *American Apartheid*, pp. 84, 97–98.

75. Morrison, *Playing*, p. 46.

76. See the discussion of' "idealizing" abstractions in Onora O'Neill,

"Justice, Gender, and International Boundaries," in *The Quality of Life*, ed. Martha Nussbaum and Amartya Sen (Oxford: Clarendon Press, 1993), pp. 303–23.

77. Patricia J. Williams, *The Alchemy of Race and Rights* (Cambridge: Harvard University Press, 1991), pp. 116, 49.

78. Bill E. Lawson, "Moral Discourse and Slavery," in Howard McGary and Bill E. Lawson, *Between Slavery and Freedom: Philosophy and American Slavery* (Bloomington: Indiana University Press, 1992), pp. 71–89.

79. Anita L. Allen, "Legal Rights for Poor Blacks," in *The Underclass Question*, ed. Bill E. Lawson (Philadelphia: Temple University Press, 1992), pp. 117–39.

80. Rawls, *Theory of Justice*; Robert Nozick, *Anarchy, State, and Utopia* (New York: Basic Books, 1974).

81. Isaacs, "Color," p. 235.

82. Earl Miner, "The Wild Man through the Looking Glass," in Dudley and Novak, *Wild Man*, pp. 89–90.

83. Jordan, *White over Black*, p. 254.

84. Drinnon, *Facing West*, p. xvii. But see Allen, *Invention of the White Race*, for the contrasting position that the Irish were indeed made nonwhite.

85. Noel Ignatiev, *How the Irish Became White* (New York: Routledge, 1995).

86. See John W. Dower, *War without Mercy: Race and Power in the Pacific War* (New York: Pantheon Books, 1986).

87. Gary Y. Okihiro, "Is Yellow Black or White?" in *Margins and Mainstreams: Asians in American History and Culture* (Seattle: University of Washington Press, 1994), pp. 31–63.

88. Sir Robert Filmer, *Patriarcha and Other Writings*, ed. Johann P. Sommerville (Cambridge: Cambridge University Press, 1991).

89. Again, it could be argued that a better formulation is to say that actually, by the terms of the Racial Contract, they are *not* the same crime, that the identity conditions change with the perpetrator, so that there is really no inconsistency. The judgment of inconsistency presupposes the background of the *social* contract.

90. According to the NAACP Legal Defense and Educational Fund in New York, of the 380 people executed since the reinstatement of

capital punishment, only 5 were whites convicted of killing blacks.

91. William Brandon, *The American Heritage Book of Indians* (New York: Dell, 1964), p. 327, quoted in Jan P. Nederveen Pieterse, *Empire and Emancipation: Power and Liberation on a World Scale* (New York: Praeger, 1989), p. 313.

92. Kiernan, *Lords*, pp. 198, 47.

93. Locke, *Second Treatise*, p. 274.

94. Ralph Ginzburg, ed., *100 Years of Lynchings* (1962; rpt. Baltimore: Black Classic Press, 1988).

95. C. J. Dashwood, quoted in Price, *White Settlers*, p. 114. One white settler, "in revenge for having been speared, had shot on sight 37 natives." Ibid., p. 115.

96. Frederick Douglass, *Narrative of the Life of Frederick Douglass, an American Slave* (New York: Viking Penguin, 1982), p. 135.

97. Carter G. Woodson, *The Mis-Education of the Negro* (1933; rpt. Nashville, Tenn.: Winston-Derek, 1990).

98. James Baldwin, *Nobody Knows My Name: More Notes of a Native Son* (1961; rpt. New York: Vintage International, 1993), p. 96.

99. Pieterse, *Empire and Emancipation*, p. 317.

100. Quoted from *Survival International Review* 4, no. 2 (1979), in Moody, *Indigenous Voice*, p. 248.

101. Jerry Gambill, "Twenty-one Ways to 'Scalp' an Indian," 1968 speech, in Moody, *Indigenous Voice*, pp. 293–95, quoted from *Akwesasne Notes* 1, no. 7 (1979).

102. Fanon, *Black Skin*.

103. *Blackisms*, quoted from *Mureena*, Aboriginal Student Newspaper, 2, no. 2 (1972), in Moody, *Indigenous Voice*, pp. 290–92.

104. Ngũgĩ wa Thiong'o, *Decolonising the Mind: The Politics of Language in African Literature* (London: James Currey, 1986), pp. 3, 12.

CHAPTER 3. "NATURALIZED" MERITS

1. Susan Moller Okin, *Women in Western Political Thought* (1979; rpt. Princeton: Princeton University Press, 1992).

2. For Hume, see the 1753–54 edition of his essay, "Of National Characters," quoted, for example, in Jordan, *White over Black*, p. 253; Georg Wilhelm Friedrich Hegel, Introduction to *The Philosophy of History*, trans. John Sibree (New York: Dover, 1956), pp. 91–99. For a detailed critique of Locke and Mill in particular, and their "colonial liberalism," see Bhikhu Parekh, "Decolonizing Liberalism," in *The End of "Isms"? Reflections on the Fate of Ideological Politics after Communism's Collapse*, ed. Aleksandras Shtromas (Cambridge, Mass.: Blackwell, 1994), pp. 85–103; and Bhikhu Parekh, "Liberalism and Colonialism: A Critique of Locke and Mill," in *The Decolonization of Imagination: Culture, Knowledge and Power*, ed. Jan P. Nederveen Pieterse and Bhikhu Parekh (London: Zed Books, 1995), pp. 81–98.

3. To be fair to Mill, he does have a famous exchange with Thomas Carlyle on the treatment of blacks in the British West Indies, in which he comes out for "progressive" (relatively, of course) social policies. See *Thomas Carlyle: The Nigger Question; John Stuart Mill: The Negro Question*, ed. Eugene R. August (New York: Appleton-Century-Crofts, Crofts Classics, 1971). But the difference is basically between less and more humane colonial policies; colonialism itself as a politico-economic system of exploitation is not being challenged.

4. Alvin I. Goldman, "Ethics and Cognitive Science," *Ethics* 103 (1993): 337–60. For further reading on the developing dialogue between the two, see *Mind and Morals: Essays on Ethics and Cognitive Science*, ed. Larry May, Marilyn Friedman, and Andy Clark (Cambridge: MIT Press, 1996).

5. Cf. Frankenberg, *White Women*, who distinguishes between the older discourse of essentialist racism, "with its emphasis on race difference understood in hierarchical terms of essential, biological inequality," and the current discourse of essential "sameness," "color-blindness," "a color-evasive and power-evasive" language that asserts that "we are all the same under the skin," which in ignoring the "structural and institutional dimensions of racism" implies that "materially, we have the same chances in U.S. society," so that "any failure to achieve is therefore the fault of people of color themselves" (pp. 14, 139).

6. For example, Donald Kinder and Lynn Sanders conclude in their analysis of American attitudes on race that on many issues of public policy, "[individual] self-interest turns out to be quite unimportant." What matter are *group* interests, "interests that are collective rather than personal," involving perceptions of deprivation as *relative*, "based less in objective condition and more in social comparison," i.e., the notion of "group relative disadvantage." And races, it turns out, are the most important social group, since race "creates divisions more notable than any other in American life": "Insofar as interests figure prominently in white opinion on race, it is through the threats blacks appear to pose to whites' collective well-being, not their personal welfare." *Divided by Color*, pp. 262–64, 252, 85.

7. Susan V. Opotow, ed., "Moral Exclusion and Injustice," *Journal of Social Issues*, 46, special issue (1990): 1, quoted in Wilmer, *Indigenous Voice*.

8. See, for a discussion, Cheryl I. Harris, "Whiteness as Property," *Harvard Law Review* 106 (1993): 1709–91; and Welchman, "Locke on Slavery."

9. Consider the "racial etiquette" of the Old South, as documented in John Dollard's *Caste and Class in a Southern Town*, 3d ed. (1937; rpt. New York: Doubleday Anchor, 1957), and explored, say, in William Faulkner's novels and Richard Wright, "The Ethics of Living Jim Crow" (1937), in *Bearing Witness: Selections from African-American Autobiography in the Twentieth Century*, ed. Henry Louis Gates Jr. (New York: Pantheon Books, 1991), pp. 39–51.

10. Kiernan cites the view held by many whites about slavery that "Negroes have far duller nerves and are less susceptible to pain than Europeans." *Lords*, p. 199.

11. Ralph Ellison, *Invisible Man* (1952; rpt. New York: Vintage Books, 1972), pp. 3, 14.

12. Baldwin, *Nobody Knows*, p. 172; James Baldwin, *The Fire Next Time* (1963; rpt. New York: Vintage International, 1993), pp. 53–54.

13. Drinnon, *Facing West*, pp. 138–39.

14. W. E. H. Stanner, *After the Dreaming* (Sydney: Boyer Lectures,

1968), p. 25, quoted in Hartwig, "Aborigines and Racism" in Stevens, *Racism* 2:10.

15. Gordon, *Bad Faith*, pp. 8, 75, 87.

16. David Stannard, *American Holocaust*. The standard response to this accusation is to claim that the vast majority of Native Americans were actually killed by disease rather than warfare or general mistreatment. Stannard replies that: no factual evidence has been presented to back up this standard claim, and even if it were true, culpability would still remain, along the same lines that we hold the Nazis morally responsible for Jewish deaths from disease, malnutrition, and overwork in the ghettos and the camps. It is estimated by some scholars that more than two million Jews actually died from these causes rather than from gassing or shooting. See, for example, Raul Hilberg, *The Destruction of the European Jews*, rev. and definitive ed., 3 vols. (New York: Holmes and Meier, 1985); and Arno Mayer, *Why Did the Heavens Not Darken! The "Final Solution" in History*, with a new foreword (1988; rpt. New York: Pantheon, 1990). Nonetheless we do, of course—as we should—assign blame for these deaths to Nazi policy, as ultimately causally responsible. For rival positions in this often angry debate, see David E. Stannard, "Uniqueness as Denial: The Politics of Genocide Scholarship" (where these points are made and these sources cited), and Steven T. Katz, "The Uniqueness of the Holocaust: The Historical Dimension," both in *Is the Holocaust Unique! Perspectives on Comparative Genocide*, ed. Alan S. Rosenbaum (Boulder, Colo.: Westview Press, 1996): 163–208 and 19–38. See also Tzvetan Todorov, *The Conquest of America: The Question of the Other*, trans. Richard Howard (1982; rpt. New York: Harper and Row, 1984), esp. chap. 3, "Love," pp. 127–82.

17. Drinnon, *Facing West*, p. 199.

18. See Stannard, *American Holocaust*, pp. 317–18.

19. E. D. Morel, *The Black Man's Burden* (1920; rpt. New York: Monthly Review Press, 1969). The same estimate is given by Jan Vansina, professor emeritus of history and anthropology at the University of Wisconsin.

20. Stannard, *American Holocaust*, p. 121. Jonathan Swift in *Gulliver's Travels* (1726) has his protagonist make shoes and a canoe

out of the skins of the subhuman/human Yahoos of part 4 (themselves based on the "Hottentots," the Khoi-khoi people of South
Africa). The sail of the canoe was "likewise composed of the
Skins of the same Animal; but I made use of the youngest I
could get, the older being too tough and thick." Jonathan Swift,
Gulliver's Travels (New York: Oxford University Press, 1977),
p. 284.

21. Clive Turnbull, "Tasmania: The Ultimate Solution," in Stevens,
Racism 2.228–34.

22. Dower, *War without Mercy*, chap. *3*, "War Hates and War
Crimes," pp. 33–73.

23. C. L. R. James, *The Black Jacobins: Toussaint L'Ouverture and
the San Domingo Revolution*, 2d ed. (1938; rpt. New York: Vintage Books, 1963), pp. 12–13.

24. Ida Wells-Barnett, *On Lynchings* (New York: Arno Press, 1969);
Ginzburg, *100 Years*.

25. Daniel R. Headrick, *The Tools of Empire: Technology and European Imperialism in the Nineteenth Century* (New York: Oxford
University Press, 1981), pp. 102–3. The bullet was so named
because it was manufactured at a British factory at Dum-Dum,
outside Calcutta.

26. Sven Lindqvist, *"Exterminate All the Brutes,"* trans. Joan Tate
(1992; rpt. New York: New Press, 1996), pp. 36–69; and see also
Ellis, *Machine Gun*, chap. 4, "Making the Map Red," pp. 79–109.
Lindqvist points out (p. 46) that an additional sixteen thousand
Sudanese were wounded in the "battle," and few or none of them
survived either, being summarily executed in its aftermath.

27. Dower, *War without Mercy*, pp. 37–38.

28. Hilberg, *Destruction of the European Jews*; Ian Hancock, "Responses to the Porrajmos: The Romani Holocaust," in Rosenbaum, *Holocaust*, pp. 39–64; Christopher Simpson, *Blowback:
America's Recruitment of Nazis and Its Effects on the Cold War*
(New York: Weidenfeld and Nicolson, 1988), chap. 2, "Slaughter
on the Eastern Front," pp. 12–26.

29. Quoted in Michael Bilton and Kevin Sim, *Four Hours in My Lai*
(New York: Penguin, *1992*), p. 336. One popular Saigon graffito
of the time was "Kill a Gook for Calley," and telegrams to the
White House ran a hundred to one in his favor. There was also

a hit song in his honor: "The Battle Hymn of Lt. Calley." *Four Hours*, pp. 338–40. For Algeria, see Fanon, *Wretched of the Earth;* and Rita Maran, *Torture: The Role of Ideology in the French-Algerian War* (New York: Praeger, 1989). Maran's conclusion is that the widespread use of torture by the French troops (in violation of French law) was made possible by the *mission civilisatrice*, since, after all, Western civilization was at stake. In Vietnam, by contrast, American troops committing atrocities simply appealed to the well-established moral principle of the M.G.R.—the "mere gook rule." See Drinnon, *Facing West*, pp. 454–59.

30. Mayer, *Why Did the Heavens?* pp. 15–16. Mayer is reporting rather than endorsing this view, since his own account seeks to locate the "Judeocide" in the context of Hitler's anticommunism and the extreme violence in Europe during and after the Great War. His explanation is a purely internalist one, jumping three centuries from the Thirty Years' War (1618–48) to the aftermath of the Great War, with no attention paid to the racial violence inflicted by Europe on non-Europe in the interim. But in our own century, just before World War I, there were the examples of the Belgian-made holocaust in the Congo and the Germans' own genocide of the Hereros after the 1904 uprising.

31. Simpson, *Blowback*, p. 5.

32. Aimé Césaire, *Discourse on Colonialism*, trans. Joan Pinkham (1955; rpt. New York: Monthly Review Press, 1972), p. 14.

33. Kiernan, *Imperialism*, p. 101.

34. Robert Harris, *Fatherland* (1992; rpt. New York: Harper Paperbacks, 1993).

35. Bartolomé de Las Casas, *The Devastation of the Indies: A Brief Account*, trans. Herma Briffault (New York: Seabury Press, 1974).

36. Stannard, *American Holocaust;* Bruni Höfer, Heinz Dieterich, and Klaus Meyer, eds., *Das Fünfhundert-jährige Reich* (Médico International, 1990); Lindqvist, *"Exterminate All the Brutes,"* pp. 160, 172.

37. Norman G. Finkelstein, *Image and Reality of the Israel-Palestine Conflict* (London: Verso, 1995), p. 93.

38. Adolf Hitler, 1932 speech, in *The Years 1932 to 1934*, vol. 1 of

Hitler: Speeches and Proclamations, 1932–1945, ed. Max Domarus, trans. Mary Fran Gilbert (1962; rpt. Wauconda, Ill.: Bolchazy-Carducci, 1990), p. 96. For this reference, I am indebted to Finkelstein, *Image and Reality*, pp. 93–94. Finkelstein points out that many of Hitler's biographers emphasize how frequently he invoked as a praiseworthy model to be emulated the successful North American extermination of the "red savages."

39. Locke, *Second Treatise*, pp. 346–49.
40. David Hume, "Of the Original Contract" (1748), anthologized, e.g., in Barker, *Social Contract*, pp. 147–66.
41. There is now an American journal with the title *Race Traitor: A Journal of the New Abolitionism*. For a collection of articles from it, see *Race Traitor*, ed. Noel Ignatiev and John Garvey (New York: Routledge, 1996).
42. Maran, *Torture*, p. 125 n. 30.
43. The slogan of *Race Traitor*.
44. Quoted in Drinnon, *Facing West*, p. 163, from the nineteenth-century American novelist Robert Montgomery Bird.
45. Chomsky, *Year 501*, p. 31.
46. Roger Moody, Introduction (to the first edition), *Indigenous Voice*, p. xxix.
47. Bilton and Sim, *Four Hours*, pp. 135–41, 176–77, 204–5.
48. W. E. B. Du Bois, *The Souls of Black Folk* (1903; rpt. New York: New American Library, 1982).
49. Sitting Bull, quoted in Moody, *Indigenous Voice*, p. 355; Churchill, *Fantasies*; David Walker, *Appeal to the Coloured Citizens of the World* (Baltimore, Md.: Black Classic Press, 1993), pp. 33, 48; Du Bois, *Souls*, pp. 122, 225; W. E. B. Du Bois, "The Souls of White Folk," in *W. E. B. Du Bois: A Reader*, ed. David Levering Lewis (New York: Henry Holt, 1995), p. 456; Richard Wright, "The Ethics of Living Jim Crow"; Marcus Garvey, *The Philosophy and Opinions of Marcus Garvey*, vols. 1 and 2, ed. Amy Jacques-Garvey (1923, 1925; rpt. New York: Atheneum, 1992), Jawaharlal Nehru, *The Discovery of India* (1946; rpt. New York: Anchor Books, 1959), quoted in Chomsky, *Year 501*, p. 20; Martin Luther King Jr., *Why We Can't Wait* (1963; rpt. New York: Mentor, 1964), p. 82; Malcolm X, 8 April 1964 speech on "Black Revolution," in *I Am Because We Are: Readings in Black Phi-*

losophy, ed. Fred Lee Hord (Mzee Lasana Okpara) and Jonathan Scott Lee (Amherst: University of Massachusetts Press, 1995), pp. 277–78; Fanon, *Wretched*, pp. 40–42; Césaire, *Discourse*, pp. 20–21; "Statement of Protest," in Moody, *Indigenous Voice*, p. 360.

50. "Knox was an influential figure in the development of British 'race science'—perhaps the most influential at mid-century—whom Darwin cites with respect if not absolute approval." Patrick Brantlinger, "'Dying Races': Rationalizing Genocide in the Nineteenth Century," in Pieterse and Parekh, *The Decolonization of Imagination*, p. 47.

51. Lindqvist, *"Exterminate,"* pts. 2 and 4; and Brantlinger, "'Dying Races.'"

52. Quoted in Cook, *Colonial Encounters*, p. 1.

53. Kiernan, *Imperialism*, p. 146. See also Okihiro, chap. 5, "Perils of the Body and Mind," in *Margins and Mainstreams*, pp. 118–47.

54. Kiernan, *Lords*, pp. 171, 237.

55. Madison Grant, *The Passing of the Great Race; or, The Racial Basis of European History* (New York: Scribner's, 1916); Lothrop Stoddard, *The Rising Tide of Color against White World-Supremacy* (New York: Scribner's, 1920). For a discussion, see Thomas F. Gossett, *Race: The History of an Idea in America* (1963; rpt. New York: Schocken, 1965), chap. 15. Gossett points out that Stoddard's book turns up in F. Scott Fitzgerald's *Great Gatsby*, disguised as *The Rise of the Colored Empires*.

56. Kiernan, *Lords*, p. 27.

57. Quoted in Dower, *War without Mercy*, p. 160.

58. Kiernan, *Lords*, pp. 319–20.

59. Ibid., p. 69.

60. Drinnon, *Facing West*, pp. 313–14.

61. Dower, *War without Mercy*, pp. 173–78.

62. Okihiro, "Perils," pp. 133, 129.

63. W. E. B. Du Bois, "To the Nations of the World," and "The Negro Problems" (1915), both in Lewis, *Du Bois*, pp. 639, 48.

64. Richard Wright, *The Color Curtain: A Report on the Bandung Conference* (1956; rpt. Jackson: University Press of Mississippi, 1994).

65. See Moody, *Indigenous Voice*, pp. 498–505.

66. Leon Poliakov, *The Aryan Myth: A History of Racist and Nation-alist Ideas in Europe*, trans. Edmund Howard (1971; rpt. New York: Basic Books, 1974), p. 5.

67. Douglass, *Narrative*, p. 107.

68. Baldwin, *Nobody Knows*, pp. 67–68.

69. See Eric R. Wolf, *Europe and the People without History* (Berkeley: University of California Press, 1982).

70. Young, *White Mythologies*.

71. See, for example, Edward Blyden's *A Vindication of the African Race* (1857).

72. See Russell et al., *The Color Complex*.

73. For the long history of the systematic evasion of race by the most famous theorists of American political culture, see Rogers M. Smith, "Beyond Tocqueville, Myrdal, and Hartz: The Multiple Traditions in America," *American Political Science Review* 87 (1993): 549–66. Smith points out (pp. 557–58) that "the cumulative effect of these persistent failures to lay out the full pattern of civic exclusion has been to make it all too easy for scholars to conclude that egalitarian inclusiveness has been the norm," whereas "the exceptions obviously have great claim to be ranked as rival norms."

74. Or at least my preferred version does. As earlier mentioned, racist versions of the "Racial Contract" are possible; these would take whites to be *intrinsically* exploitative beings who are biologically motivated to set up the contract.

75. For representative works in *legal* theory, the original home of the term, see Delgado, *Critical Race Theory*; and Kimberlé Crenshaw, Neil Gotanda, Gary Peller, and Kendall Thomas, eds., *Critical Race Theory: The Key Writings That Formed the Movement* (New York: New Press, 1995). The term, however, is now beginning to be used more widely.

76. Quoted in Dower, *War without Mercy*, p. 161.

77. *Boston Globe* article by the Japan historian Herbert Bix, 19 April 1992, quoted by Chomsky, *Year 501*, p. 239. See also James Yin and Shi Young, *The Rape of Nanking: An Undeniable History in Photographs*, ed. Ron Dorfman and Shi Young (Chicago: Innovative Publishing Group, 1996).

78. Dower, *War without Mercy,* chap. 10, "Global Policy with the Yamato Race as Nucleus," pp. 262–90.

79. For a critique from the Left, see, for example, David Harvey, *The Condition of Postmodernity: An Enquiry into the Origins of Cultural Change* (Oxford: Basil Blackwell, 1990).

80. Jürgen Habermas, *The Philosophical Discourse of Modernity: Twelve Lectures,* trans. Frederick Lawrence (Cambridge: MIT Press, 1987). For critiques, see, for example, Dussel, *Invention of the Americas;* and Outlaw, "Life-Worlds, Modernity, and Philosophical Praxis."

81. O'Neill, "Justice."

82. Richard R. Wright Jr. (not the novelist), "What Does the Negro Want in our Democracy?" in 1910–1932: *From the Emergence of the N.A.A.C.P. to the Beginning of the New Deal,* vol. 3 of *A Documentary History of the Negro People in the United States,* ed. Herbert Aptheker (Secaucus, N.J.: Citadel Press, 1973), pp. 285–93.

83. Henry Louis Gates Jr., *The Signifying Monkey: A Theory of African-American Literary Criticism* (New York: Oxford University Press, 1988), pp. xxi, xxiii, 47, 49.

84. Henry Louis Gates Jr., "Writing 'Race' and the Difference It Makes," in Gates, ed., *"Race," Writing, and Difference* (Chicago: University of Chicago Press, 1986), pp. 1–20.

85. Anthony H. Richmond, *Global Apartheid: Refugees, Racism, and the New World Order* (Toronto: Oxford University Press, 1994).